T0277518

FLAMENGO

Stephen Brandt

FLAMENGO

Winning all
the Cups

First published by Pitch Publishing, 2023

Pitch Publishing
9 Donnington Park,
85 Birdham Road,
Chichester,
West Sussex,
PO20 7AJ
www.pitchpublishing.co.uk
info@pitchpublishing.co.uk

A CIP catalogue record is available for this book
from the British Library.

ISBN 978 1 80150 453 9

Typesetting and origination by Pitch Publishing
Printed and bound in Great Britain by TJ Books, Padstow

Contents

For the football supporter —

you are the club legend

Foreword

STEPHEN IS SOMEONE who is passionate about football in every corner of the globe. He is particularly fascinated by historical football stories and over the last few years, he has educated me and many others about the history of some of the world's greatest football clubs.

From World Cup classics to FA Cup shocks. From Copa América brilliance to NASL nostalgia. From Clough and Taylor to Di Stéfano and Puskás. Stephen has an eye for a historical footballing tale supplemented with hours upon hours of research.

In this latest book, he will take you on a journey through the illustrious history of Clube de Regatas do Flamengo. You will find out which sport inspired the foundation of Flamengo as a footballing entity. You will discover a litany of historic footballers who have passed through the doors of the club, as well as being given an insight into the fierce rivalries that the club holds with particular competitors. You will be taken on a journey through Brazilian football history. Sit back, relax and enjoy the story of Flamengo and their standing in the beautiful game. *Joga bonito.*

Callum McFadden
Football Writers' Association

9

Prologue – Early Days of Brazil

BRAZIL CAN claim six world titles in the Intercontinental Cup era (1960–2004) and four in the Club World Cup era (2004–present).[1] The term world champion in sports is used so loosely that people tend to brush it off. The term in the sport of football has an even wider definition, but for now let's stick with the dictionary: 'someone who has won a competition open to people throughout the whole world'.[2] For the simple description of the sport, that's how you can describe the 1981 season for Flamengo in Brazil. They won the state, the league, the continent and the world titles in one year. Along the way they captured the hearts of many. Before we get there, a detour into a brief talk on how Brazil was founded, with an aside of the sport coming to the country.

Christopher Columbus's much-disputed discovery of the Americas was a big deal around Europe when the Portuguese stumbled upon Brazil very much the same way. There is some research that shows that the Vikings discovered the Americas years before Columbus. In 1498, Vasco da Gama, the football club named for the same, sailed

---

1   www.conmebol.com/es/19082015-1742/las-competiciones-oficiales-de-la-conmebol

2   www.collinsdictionary.com/us/dictionary/english/world-champion

from Portugal around the southern tip of Africa to India. This was what Columbus had hoped for, and da Gama established an overseas route between Europe and Asia. Two years later in 1500, Pedro Álvares Cabral set out from Portugal to replicate da Gama's journey to India, but got off-track and was on the shores of Brazil when he made land. Cabral only stayed in Brazil a few days before going off to India, but sent a letter back to the Portuguese king to tell him of the discovery. In the letter, he goes on to talk about peaceful exchanges with indigenous people who hunted with bows and arrows. We cannot be sure how the indigenous actually received the Portuguese because all the reports we get are from the invaders.

They did not find an advanced civilisation with precious metals to plunder, or a colony of social discipline like the Spanish did in Mexico and Peru. The Brazilian Indians were of the hunter-gatherer mould, though there was a subset of the culture who were moving towards agricultural society. Those who were moving towards this society were using slash-and-burn techniques to clear the land. Their technology and resources were very limited, if not primeval. This was a Stone Age society, where men and women were hunting game and fish, naked without the basic European sensibilities. There weren't even any towns, so the Portuguese had a lot of work to do.

It was apparent during the middle of the first century of settlement that it was difficult to use Indians as slave labour. They were not docile, and succumbed to western diseases at a high rate. Many tribes were completely wiped off the face of the earth by the endless devastating epidemics coming from the colonial world. Tens of thousands were killed due to smallpox, measles, tuberculosis, typhoid, dysentery and influenza. So the Brazilian Indians suffered the same type of treatment that the North American Indians faced: they were just pushed on to the fringe of society.

The explorers believed that the indigenous would be easily converted to Catholicism once the language barrier had been overcome. Even though the Pope had forbidden enslavement of natives in 1537, that didn't stop the explorers coming in and capturing the natives to sell them into slavery. The missionaries would help to protect the indigenous communities from enslavement, while, as natural, some would exploit the communities for labour. While the Portuguese thought the indigenous were harmless, there were accounts by people who saw a different picture, one focused heavily on the practice of ritual cannibalism. This rumour was used as justification for the enslavement.

Soon, sugar took over from brazilwood as the colony's most exported industry. Europeans forced enslaved Africans to work on sugar-cane plantations, reaping the money for the owners. The sugar industry attracted the Dutch, who made their way to the north-east of Brazil from 1630 to 1654. They were there for a short period, but it produced a substantial number of artworks. Governor Johan Maurits van Nassau was a supporter of scientific exploration, and placed in the capital of Maurisstad, now called Recife, botanical gardens, a zoo and two Dutch painters, Albert Eckhout and Frans Post.

As it was hard to get the natives to do anything, consequently the Portuguese turned to violent persuasion. The enslavement of the natives shaped much of the history that followed, just like in Mexico, Peru and the United States. The Portuguese played very dirty, using the vendettas the natives were using against them. When the natives were fighting for land and resources, they used the vendettas system. That was where captives were sought, and some were cannibalised. The Portuguese used this to control slaves. The history and conquering of Brazil has been whitewashed by the Brazilian elites, but needless to say, it was very rough. The wars and pestilence were horrible.

Another problem the Portuguese had in Brazil was gaining a profit from the exports. The revenue was small, only about 3 per cent, where most of the gains came from sugar in the north-east. There was also some cattle ranching that provided the food necessary for the sugar plantations. Soon, the Caribbean was leading exports in sugar so the Portuguese had to think in broader terms. In the late 1600s and early 1700s there were the discoveries of gold and diamonds respectively. This caused mass immigration from Europe into the diamond and gold regions of the country. Most of the immigration and prosperity was in Minas Gerais, and you can see it in the elaborate buildings and churches still standing.

The gold industry peaked around 1750 with production of around 15 tons a year. The total amount was between 800 and 850 tons of gold in the 18th century. Because of this, and the 1755 earthquake in Lisbon, the Portuguese finances were in deep trouble. To help these finances, the Portuguese prime minister, Pombal, expelled the Jesuits from Brazil and sold the lands to wealthy landowners. Brazil turned to agricultural exports; by independence in 1822 the three main exports were cotton, sugar and coffee. Coffee was grown in the south-east, and in the north-east, sugar and cotton.

At the end of the colonial period, half the population of Brazil were slaves. The life of a slave was hard; you were worked to death after years of service and a bad diet. The other half of the population enjoyed high incomes. So you can see the disparity right there. Land ownership was concentrated on slave owners, creating an unequal distribution of property.

The process of independence is generally very hard; much blood has been spilled over the repressed getting their lands any which way they can. However, in Brazil it was particularly smooth. In 1808 the Portuguese queen and the regent fled to Rio de Janeiro to escape the French invasion of Portugal. They brought with them 10,000 of the establishment, the aristocracy, the bureaucracy and the military to set up a government to run both countries. After the Napoleonic Wars, the two countries split without too much problem, with Brazil becoming independent with an emperor who was the son of the Portuguese monarch.

Brazil ceased paying tribute to Portugal, though they had to pay a higher internal tax burden. By gaining independence, the country could create its own banking system, print money and create a capitalist market. That's not to say that foreign capital wasn't flowing in; it was mostly in the form of direct loans to the government of Brazilian government bonds. The British took over as protectorate after the Portuguese left, and there wasn't any default on this debt so they remained in good standing with the British. In 1844 when Brazil regained its customs autonomy, measures were put in place to help stimulate the growth of raw materials. This caused the stimulation of the cotton-spinning and weaving industry. This helped provide revenue upwards of two thirds of the government's taxes, which protected the local industry.

In 1833 the United Kingdom abolished slavery in the West Indies,[3] then between 1840 and 1851 the inflow of slaves to Brazil was large, but soon after, the British Navy brought an end to that. Slavery in Brazil continued for almost four more decades. Finally, in 1888 slavery was abolished, without any compensation or help for the slaves.

In 1889 the emperor was deposed by the military, also separating the church and state. The role of the president was prearranged between politicians from either São Paulo or Minas Gerais. The monarchy had centralised power; now it was all based in the states. Some of the power was in the form of control over customs duties which could be levied on foreign and interstate commerce. State-level politics was controlled by a small political class who favoured cronyism and their relatives.

In the early years of the republic the attempts to move from slave to wage labour were strained. Coffee was not profitable around Rio because it had switched to cattle raising. So coffee started to be grown in Rio, because the climate and the soil were better there. The state government of Rio subsidised immigration, mainly based on Italians, on a massive scale from 1880 to 1928. The education level of the immigrants was higher than the native-born Brazilians, with twice the literacy rate. The wages the immigrants pulled in were also higher, but the productivity was higher still.

Portuguese rule in Brazil had several lasting consequences:[4]

---

3   www.nationalarchives.gov.uk/caribbeanhistory/slavery-negotiating-freedom.htm

4   www.theworldeconomy.org/impact/The_Portuguese_in_Brazil.html

a) Brazil is characterised by very wide disparities in income, wealth, education and economic opportunity. Nothing else compares with this; Brazil is more extreme than Asia, Europe or North America. That's continents not countries. Hammering the point home further, the social structure is very similar to the colonial period, where there was inequality in access to property, and most of the labour force were slaves. A good majority of the population doesn't get proper education.

b) Economic disparity was a popular phrase in 2020/21 in America, and such a thing has been a problem in Brazil. These inequalities are due to skin colour but don't evoke the racial tensions that the United States or England see. Brazil tended to be different from the United States because Portuguese society in the colonial period was more influenced by the Muslim world.

c) As mentioned above, Brazil has had peaceful changes and attempts at its borders. This is something unique for Americans. The Treaty of Tordesillas in 1494 divided the Americas amicably between Portugal and Spain. That just doesn't happen throughout the world. This is without saying they were invasion-free as the Dutch occupied the north-east between 1630 and 1654. There have been minor boundary conflicts between the French and the Spanish, and the largest foreign war was with Paraguay from 1865 to 1870, but that's it. Compare this with Mexico, which has lost half of its territory due to wars with Europe and the United States.

d) It's also striking that Brazil has had pretty seamless political transitions. As mentioned above, independence was gained without a struggle, as the Portuguese prince became Emperor of Brazil in 1822. Slavery was abolished without a civil war, something most countries can't or won't say. The empire evolved into a republic without a struggle in 1889. And that's not all. The Vargas government (1930–45) began and ended with very little violence. The same could be said of the military dictatorship between 1964 and 1985.

Brazil was the major inroad to South America for the British in the late 19th and 20th centuries. So we see why there was a brief history of the founding of Brazil. Most of this was due to the abundance of natural resources. However, in all of this, Britain never settled in Brazil. There were a few Britons living there, mostly important figures, diplomats, bankers and engineers, which meant that British culture was being circulated through an informal part of their empire.

So wherever the British go, football goes with them. Sometimes, it's one of their member countries that does the job. When you see the spread of the sport in South America, the United Kingdom countries are involved. The Scottish helped bring the sport to Argentina. During the Victorian and colonial eras football was thought of as a low-class sport, and rugby was the high-class sport. The guy who is widely considered the father of the sport in Brazil is Charles William Miller.

Charles William Miller was born in Brazil to a Brazilian-English mother. By the time he was school age he was sent back to Southampton. He went to Southampton's Banister Court School where he played sports. When Charles came back to Brazil he had the Hampshire FA rule book, ideas on the sport and a deflated ball. Back in England, he was not only good at football, he was also a good cricketer. However, he showed his football talent at Corinthian and St. Mary's, nowadays known as Southampton.

Like with anyone returning to South America, Miller got off the boat and then he gathered a group of players on a patch of land that would have to pass as a pitch. It was here with his deflated ball where he taught people the rules of the sport. Yes, for the sport to grow he acquired the necessary air to expand the ball. Miller's influence went beyond arranging a basic kickabout with a group of people. He was from an educated, well-to-do family and had the contacts to communicate and organise on a large scale.

The process went to a grand scale when he, on 13 May 1888, set up São Paulo Athletic Club, which to this day is still around. He did not stop there. He laid the foundation for the Liga Paulista, the first organised tournament in the country. The sport didn't take the consistency of the British game; the flow and grace of the people in Brazil took over, as the game developed depending on the air of the country it was being played in.

And the sport caught on quickly, but Miller wasn't the only person to bring it to the shores of Brazil. Scottish textile worker Thomas Donohoe helped spread the sport in the country too. Like with a lot of things in the sport, there's not much information to flesh out Donohoe's life. The club historian at Bangu Atlético Clube is trying to change all of that because that's where Donohoe started out. The Scot arrived in an area that was very small; it had a single street and a textile factory. Donohoe liked what he settled into, but he wanted to bring football back into his life. He was disgusted to see that there weren't any teams in the neighbourhoods. That makes sense as the natural pastimes of Bangu were cycling and music, not sport.

So the best thing for him to do was bring the game to them. He wrote to his wife Elizabeth asking her to join him in Brazil and to bring their children, and a ball. Not long after they arrived in September 1894, the first match in Brazil took place on a field next to the textile factory. According to historian Molinari, it was a six-a-side match between the workers, which was a full eight months before Charles Miller's game.

The disagreement between the two fathers of the sport concerned the rules and the official part of the match. It's the same old friendly versus official recorded game debate, as Miller's match was 11-a-side with the official association rules. Miller implanted the sport in the country, developing the first clubs and the first championships.

For Donohoe's supporters in Bangu that argument has little merit, mostly due to local pride. Since football was considered low class, the managers of the textile factory thought it would lead to degeneracy among their workers. By the time the factory owners allowed the team to form, it was 1904 and the São Paulo league was in its third season. Another first that can be put in the tale of football in the country for the people from Bangu is the first black man to play for a Brazilian club in 1905, Francisco Carregalo.

We can go further into Donohoe's life[5] to flesh out more about him. Tom Donohoe and the rest of the people emigrated from the United Kingdom in early 1894. He was the son of Irish parents and was a big man at well over 6ft tall. He was brought up with a family of seven children in Busby, an industrial village of Renfrewshire. Tom played football in the local Scottish leagues as a forward, so when he arrived in Bangu in April of 1894 he expected to continue to play. That's where he developed the six-a-side match. Eventually, the friendly matches gathered attention to a point where non-British workers would join for the now 11-a-side games.

It took a while for a club to be formed in the city, and it would take a chance meeting at the factory for it to happen. By the end of 1903, Andrew Proctor proposed a sports club that would play football in the winter and cricket in the summer – that's how Athletic Club Bangu was formed. It was mostly a Scots club run by three Scots: Tommy Donohoe as the vice-president, Andrew Proctor as secretary and treasurer, and John Stark as captain of football. Bangu's first match was in July 1904 against Rio Cricket, and Donohoe would end up playing for a club in Brazil after all. So while we have two schools of thought for the start of the sport, we can point out that it flourished no matter where it was invented.

Football came to Rio in September 1901[6] through Anglo-Brazilian Oscar Cox, who first played it while living in Sweden. Cox was a promoter of the sport and the association members in the Clube Brasileiro de Cricket, now Paysandu. He was kind of a missionary, and did work

---

5   www.scotsfootballworldwide.scot/tommydonohoe
6   *Origin Stories* – Chris Lee, p191.

that was parallel to Charles Miller, as mentioned above. In 1901, Cox and some assorted friends took a boat to Niterói to spread the sport. On 22 September, on the field of the Rio Cricket and Athletic Association (RCAA), they played an exhibition match which was the first in the state. The match ended 1-1 between a team of Brazilians and one of British expats. There was a very small number of people who attended the game, only 16, and 11 of them were members of Rio Cricket Club.

Ever the optimist, Cox and his group travelled on. In October they moved on to São Paulo where a side called Rio Team played a São Paulo team twice, 2-2 and 0-0 respectively. Both teams weren't clubs, just groups of friends, and Rio Team played the São Paulo team on 19 and 20 October. These two results against people from São Paulo motivated them to create a club in Rio. The athletes on the long train journey from São Paulo to Rio debated the idea. This idea became the Fluminense Football Club.

Flamengo's history is full of great goalscorers with numbers that put them in the legendary stratosphere. Zico was the biggest, but there were others: Dida, Henrique, Pirillo, Romário, Jarbas, Leônidas, Bebeto, Zizinho and Índio. One that is forgotten was from the early days: Claudionor Gonçalves da Silva, or Nonô, from the 1920s. Nonô was the first top scorer in the Campeonato Carioca who was part of Flamengo, and was also the first player to score 100 times for the club. He was born in Rio de Janeiro in 1899, and started playing at the now extinct Palmeiras Athletic Club. They played in Quinta da Boa Vista in São Cristóvão, in the Northern Zone.

The club reached the first division of the Carioca Championship in 1920, where they would play against

Flamengo, Botafogo, Fluminense and América. After that 1920 season, the champions Flamengo took interest in the young player. They were also looking at Orlando Torres from that squad, and they were both transferred to Flamengo on 26 March 1921. Orlando spent just three seasons at Flamengo, scoring only four goals, before transferring to Botafogo.

Players were still amateur at the time, either going to school or professionals in other aspects of life. Training was so sporadic that clubs put advertisements in newspapers for the practices. Flamengo participated in the Campeonato Carioca, which was pretty much year-round at that point. They were up against São Paulo, Minas Gerais and Rio Grande do Sul.

Nonô started scoring early in the season, getting two against Bangu in a 4-2 win, two more in a 4-0 rout over América and one in the 4-3 derby win over Fluminense. As he kept scoring, the club kept winning, and titles kept coming in. After his first title in 1921, he scored his only call-up for the Brazilian team, in the Copa América in 1921. Nonô wouldn't be there long, as he was injured during the first ten minutes of the match between Brazil and Argentina and couldn't continue.

Nonô and the club had a down 1922 season, as Flamengo finished second behind América in the Carioca, and Nonô only had seven goals; 1922 was set to be a big year, righting the wrongs of the previous one. Nonô scored in every match save for the first one, having an 18-goal season, making him the top scorer in the Carioca Championship. This was the first time the club had that distinction. However, they missed out on the title, as they would the following season as well.

The following year Nonô scored 13 times in the Campeonato Carioca, and 18 times in total. Nonô's good work didn't give them the title again. This was becoming a recurring theme for Flamengo. It wasn't until 1925 that he started breaking records. In that year he scored 29 goals in the Carioca, which is still a record almost a century later. Behind his scoring, Flamengo ran off 11 victories in 12 games. Nonô got 24 goals in the last six games, and two in a 4-0 rout over América to win the title.

Nonô left after having scored 124 goals. On 4 May 1930 he played his last match for the club, which was against Botafogo in the Carioca. He couldn't stop Flamengo from losing 2-1, but the fans still cheered him on. Sadly, on 21 July 1931 he died of tuberculosis, a poor man.

One of the things that Brazil and Rio have given to football is the bicycle kick. It's mostly Brazilians when you think of it, and Pelé. The originator of the move, like the originator of the sport, was up for debate. Until recently, many people have included Leônidas da Silva as one of the people who could have invented it. Leônidas was an explosive player whose career spanned two decades from 1930 to 1950. He was born and raised in Rio, and was known for his speed. Leônidas, at an early age, was a great scorer for Bonsucesso, where he scored 23 goals in 39 matches. It was at Bonsucesso where he employed the bicycle kick, in April 1932 in the Carioca, and put the move on display for the first time.

Five years later in 1936, Leônidas signed for Flamengo. After a great World Cup in France just a year before, he helped lead Flamengo to a Rio State Championship. Another lasting image of him in the game was that he was one of the first black players, and a great player too. One of the great, better-supported clubs in the country had a great black player; this was a major step.

As already referred to, the race issue. No matter what subject in football you read about, the sad thing is you have to talk about racism. The fact that people degrade other people based on the colour of their skin should never, ever happen. But the sport is based on elitism all the way back to its origins in England. When the elites played, the social impact was negligible. Few could access it; few cared. The sport was brought to the common people when played in the cities and factories. These types of matches were open to everyone, including the African slaves. That's where the elites had an issue. Slavery was only abolished in Brazil in 1888; it was the last country in the western world to do so.

In 1889 the Brazilian elite introduced a national programme of *branqueamento* ('whitening'). The purpose was to make the Brazilian whiter, and in doing so they would encourage white immigrants to come to Brazil and marry the natives. As if that wasn't bad enough, the Brazilian government made sure that Afro-Brazilian history was excluded from schools and public schools. People of African descent were denied jobs due to their skin colour. So in order to change all of this, what happens? Football comes around.

By the start of the 1900s, football's popularity moved from the elite classes to the masses. From 1910 players of African descent emerged in the Brazilian football scene. Such players as Arthur Friedenreich, who will be talked about later, and Joaquim Prado. However, African players straightened their hair and put rice powder on their skin to look less black. Vasco da Gama was the first team to win a league championship in Brazil with a mixed-race team. But this didn't change the game. By 1924 the league changed the rules so mixed-race clubs like Vasco were banned from competing. This didn't stay around long as the following year the mixed-race clubs were reinstated.

The rise of dictator Getúlio Vargas in 1930 started the process of the racial divisions breaking down. Vargas hoped to unite the entire nation behind his iron fist of rule. He popularised cultural elements in every class, like when he gave his endorsement of capoeira, an Afro-Brazilian martial art which had been vilified. Then he promoted samba, which at the time was a dance only associated with the poor.

While that all helped ease the race relations, in 1933 the authoritarian made football professional. This allowed a great influx of Afro-Brazilian athletes to play. As the Brazilian game got more and more Afro-Brazilian, the national team got better. Brazilians wanted a great team, regardless of their skin colour, something that Europe was still lagging far behind on. The 1950 World Cup was hosted in Brazil and has had many articles and books written about it, but it was the first South American edition of the tournament, and Brazil made its way to the final against Uruguay, and lost in a shocking manner 2-1. Barbosa, an African-Brazilian player, was blamed for the loss and saw his life spiral out of control.

The tide turned, starting in 1958 when Brazil won their first World Cup. They were able to show the doubters that an African-Brazilian team could win. It wasn't just squad players; it was greats like Pelé, Garrincha and others. Over the next decade Brazil came to dominate the game.

As is with every developing footballing nation, they had to cobble together a national team. The British again have a hand in this development, and it was a travelling club.

Just two weeks before the start of World War One in July 1914, Exeter City arrived in Brazil. The English FA had previously been invited to Argentina for a series of matches in Buenos Aires against the local clubs. Exeter were picked as the club to go, and they were a little one founded just ten years before. This was a good time for the club to make money, and they would be received as heroes on the shores of South America. For the rest of the trip, wherever they went they would get a heroes' welcome.

On 22 May 1914, 15 players left Southampton docks for their 18-day trip to Rio de Janeiro. The stay was anything but good. While they were with Santos, the entire team were arrested at a beach where bathing was banned. A British diplomat intervened in the matter and stopped the squad from being sent back to England. The players got off with a complaint about public indecency.

Exeter moved on to Argentina where they played eight friendlies. They then went to Brazil to play another three matches in Rio de Janeiro, and São Paulo. Exeter officials applied for visa extensions but the club were only able to fulfil the match in Rio. In 1914 Rio was Brazil's capital city, but São Paulo wanted to participate on the tour. So it was decided that a team made up of players from both cities would compete. This was effectively the birth of the Brazilian national team. Selecting the participants became known as *Seleção*, the Portuguese name for selection. To this day, Seleção is the nickname for the Brazilian national team.

The Seleção made its debut against Exeter at the home of Fluminense, Estádio das Laranjeiras, on 12 July 1914. As mentioned above, Exeter were treated as heroes, and the local newspapers hyped them up to extraordinary levels. They were looked upon as people coming from an unknown

27

place to spread the game. Fluminense's ground was small, and the attendance was around 10,000 people.

The local fans weren't used to seeing what was on the field, a hardness of their English opponents. Star of the time Arthur Friedenreich was met with an elbow that knocked two teeth loose. The flair and ball skills were things that the English weren't used to, and Seleção won 2-0. The winning players were carried off the pitch as national heroes.

It would be good to be able to say that Exeter came back to the shores of England and became great, but that would be a lie. Most of the players from that match went off to the trenches of World War One. Dick Pym, who fought in the war, lifted the FA Cup with Bolton in the 'White Horse Cup Final' of 1923. On 21 July 2014 Exeter and Fluminense Under-23s met in a commemorative match. The ball from the 1914 match was used to kick off the events, but then replaced for the right match ball. That ball is in Fluminense's club museum. Six hundred fans from Devon travelled to watch the match, but it ended in a 0-0 draw.

While on the point of the origins of football and the globetrotting nature of the clubs in Brazil, we have to talk about the Corinthian Football Club and how they spurned Corinthians Paulista. The original Corinthian Football Club were formed in 1882 by N.L. Jackson who was the assistant honorary secretary of the Football Association. The club were formed at the time to help England beat the Scottish national team. After all, a territory of England was experiencing too much success for England's liking, and Scotland had to be taken care of. A 6-0 loss was the final straw.

Every Scottish international at the time played for Queen's Park, then one of the top clubs. Queen's Park have always been an amateur side. So naturally, Corinthian were to be the English counterpart. Being an amateur side, the players could be picked from the greatest schools, who had the best training and education. Basically, the elite of the elite. They had to always follow the founding principles: amateurism, fair play, sportsmanship and the Corinthian Spirit. The Corinthian Spirit was playing with respect for the game, the opposition and how a gentleman plays the game. Corinthians didn't believe in the activity of scoring or saving penalties.

Within four years of the foundation of Corinthians, nine players were called up to the English national team. Twice, in 1894 and 1895, the whole team were Corinthian-based. Domestically, they defeated Manchester United 11-3 in 1904, a record score that stands to this day.

They toured the world leaving their mark, like inspiring Real Madrid to wear white. Their biggest tours were in Brazil, where in 1910 they were invited to Rio de Janeiro to face Fluminense. They also, on the tour, went to São Paulo after being contacted by former player Charles Miller. When he was a schoolboy in Southampton in 1892, Corinthian came to play a Hampshire XI, but only had ten men. So Miller was drafted in.

Corinthians went over to play Miller's side, São Paulo Athletic, on the 1910 tour. Five local railway workers were so impressed by their British visitors that they decided to make their own team. Miller suggested the name of the club after those who had inspired them. Sports Club Corinthians Paulista was born, and this was all due to a stopover on the tour after Rio and Fluminense.

Corinthians Paulista grew into a very successful club who would win Copa Libertadores, Club World Cup and domestic titles; Corinthian Football Club would slowly decline at the start of World War One. At this point the club lost ten men and counting as they found more people every year were being killed in the war. After the war Corinthians joined the FA Cup, in 1923, but lost in the first match. They never made it past the fourth round.

In 1936 they were dealt another blow as their home and the national stadium at the time, the Crystal Palace, was burned to the ground. Interest in amateur football was waning as the rise of professionalism grew. In 1939, just before World War Two, Corinthian merged with the Casuals, which they are still called today, and joined the league system. The two Corinthians still have a relationship as they have played matches against each other as recently as 2015. The South American side sells the English club's shirts on their website.

The building of the Maracanã in Rio[7] is part of the lore of the 1950 World Cup. It took two years and almost 4,000 workers to build the Maracanã, the name meaning 'green bird'. It is named after the river that flows through Rio's northern barrios. When it was opened in June of 1950, it was ready for the fourth World Cup, and was the biggest soccer stadium in the world. When filled, it was the biggest crowd football had ever seen.

The 1950 World Cup was the first since World War Two, and the first to have a British team. Even with that, the British media coverage was sparse. The newspapers relied on short news dispatches, and radio provided only brief reports. It would be a good thing, though, as the USA beat

---

7   https://medium.com/@paulbrownUK/world-cup-1950-the-maracanazo-5f737df90425

England 1-0 in Belo Horizonte. The final of the World Cup between Uruguay and Brazil on 16 July 1950 was refereed by George Reader, a schoolmaster from Southampton. Tickets for the final match were sold out of Rio's biggest department stores and were gone within a few hours. Brazil were firm favourites to win, and the newspaper *O Mundo* proclaimed Brazil champions before the match was even played. Eventually, Uruguay won, causing the dejection of many Brazilian fans. This led to the belief that when Brazil wore white shirts, they lost.

Chapter 1

The History of
Flamengo Football Club

FLAMENGO STARTED in 1895 just six years after
the Proclamation of the Republic, but not with football.
The club actually started with rowing, which was a very
popular sport then. This was practised on the beaches of
Flamengo and Botafogo, and the club were christened Clube
de Regatas do Flamengo, wearing the red and black uniform
that you see today.

Just after the founding of the club, football began to take
preference. In 1911 there was an internal disagreement within
Fluminense; some talked about leaving the club; others
spoke about leaving the sport completely. Alberto Borgerth,
a Fluminense player, made a proposal to create a football
team in Flamengo. On 8 November the football section
was created. The new team drew attention, and created
popularity by training at Praia do Russel. Flamengo's first
match was on 3 May 1912, in a 16-2 win over Mangueira.
The first line-up was: Baena, Píndar, Nery, Coriol, Gilberto,
Galo, Baiano, Amaldo, Amarante, Gustavo and Borgerth.
Gustavo, Amarante, Amaldo had four, Borgerth three and
Galo one.

Flamengo were very good right away – in 1912 they won their first Campeonato Carioca. The win came in the second to last match, 2-1 over Fluminense. Riemer scored the all-important title goal. That first football shirt they wore was *'Papagaio de Vintem'*, chequered in red and black. They did go to a horizontal-stripe kit afterwards, and as is common have changed their kit every so often to help boost shirt sales.

Going back to that first goal, we should talk about Gustavo de Carvalho.[8] That first goal, according to the club's official website, was right from the opening kick-off. In the first attack of the match from Flamengo at the opponents' goal, Gustavo took a pass from Baiano and put the ball in the back of the net. Gustavo didn't stay in football that long; he retired in 1918. He returned, being elected as president of Flamengo in 1939 and staying until 1942.

We get to move on with another great name on the ledger of Flamengo: Henry Welfare, an ex-Liverpool player.[9] The story starts back in Liverpool with his home debut against Sheffield Wednesday on 15 February 1913, deputising for Bill Lacey. While he didn't score that often, he was a good hand for the club. He did score his only goal for Liverpool at Anfield against Derby County.

Not getting any more matches at Liverpool, Welfare moved to Rio de Janeiro in August of 1913 to work as a geography and maths teacher at Ginásio Anglo-Brasileiro. The school's PE teacher, J.A. Quincey-Taylor, happened to be the first-team coach at Fluminense Football Club,

8 www.torcedores.com/noticias/2020/05/autor-de-primeiro-gol-da-historia-do-flamengo-saiu-do-maior-rival-e-marcou-cinco-vezes-na-estreia

9 www.lfchistory.net/Players/Player/Profile/879

and used Welfare's talents to their fullest for the team. It would be 20 more years before a professional league formed in Brazil, and Welfare was at the top of the scoring charts. From 1913 to 1924 they won the Campeonato Carioca, the football league of the state of Rio de Janeiro, three years on the trot, scoring 163 goals in 166 matches.

As an amateur, Welfare wasn't committed to a team so he turned out for Flamengo in their tour of Belém from December 1915 to January 1916, scoring seven goals in four games. Then in 1927 he became the coach for Vasco da Gama, and for the next ten years he was the best coach in the land.

Brazil are known for their colourful nicknames, and the use of just first names. Pelé's name is a nickname, and we talk about Ronaldo, Romário, Zico and Sócrates because of such a thing. Henry Welfare was listed as Welfare, but that was because he was English. As Alex Bellos says in *Futebol: The Brazilian Way of Life*, 'Brazilian football is an international advert for the cordiality of Brazilian life because of its players' names. Calling someone by their first name is a demonstration of intimacy, calling someone by their nickname more so.'[10]

Local players would be called by their first name, like Zico, Nunes, Júnior et al. It's just a common way Brazilians changed the game. Take any line-up from any club and you'll see the last names of the European-based players. It's always Cruyff, Keegan, Dalglish, Pelé, Zico and Ronaldo. The more and more you look at the sport, the more you see the Brazilian influence.

---

10 *Futebol: The Brazilian Way of Life* – Alex Bellos, p253.

We transition back to the tale of the Flamengo history. The beautiful game in Brazil[11] is well known worldwide. It's fashionable to own a scarf or jersey, or know their players. There are many podcasts and computer games that help people learn about the players from the past. But what if I told you there was a player before Pelé that was better? His name was Arthur Friedenreich. And yes, he was German/Brazilian.

Friedenreich, a son of a German businessman, played soccer in São Paulo. Arthur was half white, half black. Oscar, who was Arthur's father, played soccer at the Brazilian club SC Germania, which as the name infers was only for German immigrants. Arthur joined the club at 17 in 1909, which made him the first black player in history to play in the professional league. Brazilian society was very racist at the time. Blacks weren't allowed to celebrate with their club if they won a cup, and were not able to hold top jobs. Arthur would go on to play with many of the top clubs at the time: São Paulo, Flamengo, Ypiranga, Atlético Mineiro and Paulistano.

The Tiger, as he was affectionately called by the fans, did something even the great Pelé didn't do. He became the top scorer in Brazil eight times, in 1912, 1914, 1917, 1918, 1919, 1921, 1927 and 1929. Arthur was a great dribbler, would never give up on the field and had a sharp eye for goal. When he played for Paulistano when they toured Europe, his fandom stretched worldwide. By the start of the 1920s he was considered the best player in the world.

---

11 https://worldsoccertalk.com/2016/08/20/arthur-friendenreich-first-great-brazilian-player/

On the international level, his best achievement was Brazil's 1919 Copa América triumph, where he scored the winning goal against Uruguay in the 122nd minute. It was such a good goal that the boot he scored it with was paraded by fans around the streets of Rio de Janeiro. The boot was even nicknamed 'The glorious foot of Friedenreich'. It was finally put in a local jeweller's store for all to see.

He was one of those players who changed society. Very few can say that. Many players changed the game. Where he met racism and prejudice, he changed it. Where black players weren't allowed in national teams or to celebrate with their fans or team-mates, he changed that. In 1921 society was outraged when the black players were left out of the national side by the selection committee. That was because the common folk didn't see the colour of their skin; they saw their play. That was something Brazilian blacks needed. He lived the life that he could, drank expensive beer and partied when he wanted.

We cannot leave this chapter without talking about Fla–Flu and the start of the problems. The name of the rivalry comes from the two names of the clubs, Flamengo and Fluminense. Later, we will go more into this rivalry. Alberto Borgerth helped the club get started.

Borgerth was born on 3 December 1892 to a Brazilian father, Dr José de Siqueira Alvares Borgerth, who was head of security during D. Pedro II's second reign, and a Hungarian mother. He lived in his early days with the sport that was accorded to him. Alberto even rowed at Flamengo when he was 13, but never thought his career would be so intertwined with the club. In 1910 he played for Fluminense, debuting when he was only 17, in a 5-2 victory over América. Borgerth scored two goals on his debut. They didn't win the title that year, but the next season Fluminense won the Campeonato Carioca.

There was a break that caused players from Fluminense to leave. In September of 1911 the coaching staff at Fluminense decided to drop Borgerth and other players. This caused a rift between the players and the club. Borgerth took the lead on the discussion, and where there wasn't any solution, he reported that back to the rebels. The consensus of the group was to resign from the club. That led them to finding a new club, to which Flamengo were the solution. The catch in this was Flamengo were a rowing club, and lacked a football team. So in November of that year Borgerth proposed the creation of a football side of the club. The members of the club, on Christmas Eve 1911, voted to start a football club. The first training was at Russell Beach in Rio.

Alberto Borgerth came to Flamengo with Gallo, Nery, Amarante, Gustavinho, Lawrence, Baiano, Baena and Píndaro. As mentioned above, Flamengo's first match was a 16-2 win over Mangueira, with Borgerth scoring some of the goals. In that first year Flamengo captured the championship three points ahead of the second-placed club. This would be the missing piece to crown Borgerth's commitment to Flamengo. He didn't stop there, as he was part of the 1915 title-winning side, and he retired in 1916 as the first great goalscorer, putting in 21 goals in 45 matches.

Clubs get their colours in strange ways. Atlético Madrid and Athletic Bilbao were originally in Blackburn-like colours until a snafu made them switch to Southampton colours. Notts County are partly responsible for Juventus's jersey, and there are some rumours floating around that Leeds going to white jerseys was because of Real Madrid. Boca Juniors got their colours from the ships coming into the port.

Flamengo did not always play in their normal red and black. They in fact played in blue and gold, but changed to the colours you see now for a very funny reason. The salt water in Guanabara Bay made the colours run. In the early 1900s you didn't have water purifiers to make the water useable; you had to wash in a river or ocean.

So as the red and black team took the field in May 1912 to face Mangueira, they sported a kind of chequerboard top. It had red, black and white colour tones to it. The initial uniform did not bring results, and the club out of superstition stopped wearing it. Another shirt was adapted more like today's, and the club went on to great success, winning the Rio Championships of 1914 and 1915.

Then 1916 rolled around, and people noticed that the shirt reminded them of the German flag. At the time, World War One was kicking off and Germany were part of the triple alliance fighting the Entente of the British Empire, France, Russia, the United States, Portugal and a number of other countries. Brazil hadn't entered the war, but there were frequent protests in the streets of Rio de Janeiro against Germany.

So the first actual match in the red and black jerseys came against the 1914 champions São Bento. However, in 1915, even going into 1916, São Bento had not been that good. The exact date of the match seems to be lost to time, but we know English attacker Sidney Pullen scored the first goal in the new shirt. Flamengo were known at the time as a pressing team, and despite having the lead they wanted more goals. Later in the first half, Pullen put a ball into the path of Gumercindo for a 2-1 lead at half-time. That's what they ended with. The change in jerseys didn't help anything right away, as the league title would go to

América. Years later, the club would go undefeated in the 1920 season for the title.

There are few accomplishments in football better than an undefeated season. Many know about Arsenal's or Preston North End's, but few have paid attention to the Rio club in 1920. This was a busy year in Rio de Janeiro, at the time the nation's capital. The country was returning to normality after the Spanish flu pandemic ruined the world. Strangely, the flu came from Fort Riley in Kansas, which is in the United States. The carnival of 1920 was put on to bring back the joy in the city. Even the official visit of King Albert of Belgium was there to keep the people excited. However, the trip interrupted the Carioca Championship, not the last thing to be suspended for the year.

The Campeonato Carioca began on 11 April that season. Flamengo opened up the year at the Laranjeiras Stadium, drawing 0-0 with Bangu, beating Mangueira 3-0 in the semi-finals and Carregal hitting the only goal in the final against Cristóvão. Defender Píndaro, who had retired before the 1920 season, was a doctor and helped fight the Spanish flu in the city while playing for the club. Ex-Grêmio goalkeeper Júlio Kuntz would be brought in before the season. When Kuntz's time was up with Flamengo, he would be considered as one of the best in his position in the history of the club. Midfielder Rodrigo and striker João de Deus Candiota also came in.

Across the city, the sworn enemies Fluminense were coming off a golden era, winning the last three titles. They had a great line-up with Mano, Zezé, Welfare, Machado and Bacchi; they scored 68 goals in the 1919 season. The Metropolitan League of Sports Athletics (LMSA) was the organisation behind the league, which was running on a points system and had ten teams. Palmeiras had just been promoted into the top league too. Even with all of the Fluminense power, Flamengo showed their hand to conquer the title.

The first match was on 18 April at Vila Isabel, which was located in an old zoo. Flamengo were ahead 2-0, with goals from Carregal and midfielder Aníbal Candiota in the first half, before storming to a 3-1 win after a goal in the second half from Eustace Pullen. They followed up that match with one against Mangueira, who were a poor team but gave the Flamengo side all they could take. Flamengo were down 1-0 in the first half, but stormed back to 2-1 with goals from Eustace Pullen and Sisson taking it to half-time. In the second half the team started scoring in bunches. Sisson scored three more goals and Pullen scored again to make the score 6-2.

Flamengo were off and running and their next great match would be against Fluminense. This was the first time that Flamengo would play in their stadium in Rua Paissandu. Fluminense, on the other hand, were undefeated in the derby since the first edition when Flamengo won 4-1 in May of 1916. On the matchday of 1920, there were an estimated 15,000 people at the game. Sidney Pullen opened the scoring for Flamengo in the first half, and Junqueira made it two in the second. Machado put a goal in for good measure for the tricolors as Flamengo won 2-1. The victory was a great boost to the supporters of Flamengo as they invaded the pitch. This was also more proof that Flamengo could stop Fluminense's attempt at a fourth league title. A week later Flamengo tied with América 0-0.

June would only have two matches in it. The first was against São Cristóvão in Figueira de Melo under heavy rains that are common in the area. The field was flooded, but Junqueira hit three goals and Leo hit one to win 4-3. Palmeiras was the second match of June, and due to many defensive losses, Píndaro had to come out of retirement to help out in this one. Flamengo scored twice in the first half through Junqueira and Candiota to go into half-time as 2-0 leaders. In the second half, like with other matches, the scoring started flooding in. Candiota scored two more goals, and Sidney Pullen finished the scoring off to close the match at 5-0.

The club played Botafogo on 11 July. Up until then Flamengo had had six victories in six games, but hadn't faced any of the great teams. This would be the first big one for the club, and it was at Rua Paissandu. Botafogo got the scoring off to a start with a goal from Petiot but, as we know, Flamengo went undefeated, so Geraldo scored a goal in the second half and Junqueira scored the match-winner to prove that Flamengo could hang with the big boys.

Against Andarahy, Flamengo put themselves in the driver's seat for the title. Junqueira scored two goals for the 2-1 win. Flamengo kept expanding the distance between them and the rest of the pack, with the help of Fluminense and Botafogo losing. In the return match against Botafogo, Flamengo put themselves well ahead. In the first minute Sisson scored the first goal, before Vadinho tied it up for Botafogo. In the 19th minute Sidney Pullen headed in a corner kick to make it 2-1. Junqueira kicked the third goal in to put Flamengo four points ahead of Botafogo, seven over Fluminense in third. Then the matches stopped from 15 August to 31 October. Upon returning, Flamengo still had a lead, but Botafogo had trimmed it to one point, and América were in third now.

Flamengo kept winning, closing in on the title, but they still had to sweat it out as Fluminense could make a move back up the standings. They had three games in hand, and the pressure started to mount as the 14 November round saw Flamengo and Palmeiras play out a careless 1-1 draw. Realising what was happening, the club went into a match with Bangu and needed to get a point. Flamengo were one up when Junqueira, who went goalless against Palmeiras, doubled the lead. Then Claudionor made it three before the break.

In the second half, Flamengo went four up with Candiota's goal. A late goal by Machado could not keep Flamengo from winning 4-3, putting Flamengo closer to the title. On 28 November, if results fell the right way, Flamengo would be the champions. Things were coming easy for Flamengo in 1920. In the first minute Junqueira scored the first goal, and it took until the second half for Andarahy to tie the game. Seven minutes in, Gilabert scored. Flamengo had to wait until 13 minutes left in the match for Sidney Pullen to make it 2-1. Bangu later made sure that Flamengo won the title, defeating Botafogo 4-3. Eventually, Flamengo kept an unbeaten record: there were 18 games, with 13 wins and five draws. No one has done that since in Brazil. But what made it even better was that Flamengo also won the rowing crown that same year, making the club the land and sea champion.

Júlio Kuntz, as mentioned, was one of the greatest goalkeepers the club have ever had. Like a lot of people in his day, he was born from immigrants, in his case German. He was born in the state of Rio Grande do Sul in an area that became Novo Hamburgo, loosely named New Hamburg. Kuntz started his career in his town, but by May of 1917 he was in Porto Alegre with Grêmio. By the end of 1919 he was on the move again to Rio de Janeiro, to a now defunct club in Silva Manoel Football Club. With that club going away, he ended up staying in Rio.

He was now playing with Flamengo in the Metropolitan League. Kuntz was brought to the club by one of his friends who was playing for the reserve side of Flamengo. On 4 April 1920 he made his debut for the senior team. This was the second undefeated season in Flamengo's history, but was also one of the weapons to overthrow the run of Fluminense, a three-time champion. Kuntz was ever present in the matches for the title that year. For the season, he only let in 17 goals in 16 matches played.

It was a bad year for the club in 1921, despite Kuntz's great goalkeeping. They lost to Bangu 4-2, then a 4-0 win against América put them slowly back on track. In the derby against Fluminense, Kuntz was brilliant in a 4-3 win in Laranjeiras on 29 May to ensure the victory. But the bottom fell out of the side as the club stumbled between 5 June and 7 August, drawing four of six games, with one win and one loss. Eventually, they battled back and won the 1922 title over Villa Isabel 3-1, with a brace from Henry Welfare.

Kuntz stayed with the club for a few more years, leaving in 1924 for Paulistano. He eventually toured Europe to face the French, Swiss and Portuguese clubs. Many years later in 1929 Kuntz returned to Flamengo to fill in as a goalkeeper against Vasco in a friendly, and in 1931 in the Carioca Championship against São Cristóvão. He could still show the magic of years before, every now and then. In 1932 he gave up the sport and he became a referee in 1938. He never got to enjoy that career as in August of that year he passed away.

Borgerth never really left Rio, and helped the rest of the country in various areas. He was the president of the Metropolitan Football Federation in the 1950s, director of the Brazilian Sports Confederation (CBD) and a member of the Superior Court of Sports Justice (STJD). As a doctor, he helped found the Hospital Jesus in 1935 and the Hospital Miguel Couto the next year. He was a busy and diverse man.

He died on 25 November 1958 at 65. His memory and meaning to the club lives on to this day. In 2012, on the centenary celebration of the club, he was honoured by Flamengo on the back of Vágner Love's shirt in the game that marked the 100th year of the founding.

One of the most forgotten things in Flamengo's history is the Open Tournament of 1936. It symbolises a decisive moment in Rio de Janeiro and Flamengo football history, for it was the conquest of two great players for the club, Domingos da Guia and Leônidas da Silva. This was the decade of professionalism in Brazilian football. Of course, the main clubs of Rio de Janeiro – Flamengo, Fluminense, Vasco and América – split from the Metropolitan Association of Athletic Sports in 1933 to form the Liga Carioca de Futebol (LCF). So for three years, 1933–36, Rio had two championships organised by different federations. This dissent reflected what was happening nationally as the clubs that adopted professionalism created the Brazilian Football Federation, which would govern the professional side of the game.

In 1936 only seven clubs competed in the Carioca Championship organised by the LCF: Flamengo, Fluminense, América, Bonsucesso, Associação Atlética Portuguesa, Praça Eleven and Jequiá. The calendar was very short, with the number of matches for each club at 15, split into three rounds. This was insufficient to sustain the professional regime, because federations wanted as many matches as possible. Given the need to keep teams always active to generate the income for salaries, the LCF decided to create other competitions to move its members to. One was the Extra Tournament that started in 1934, and the other was the Open Tournament, which was not limited to the Carioca Championship participants.

The first edition of the Open Tournament, held in 1935, had 23 teams, mostly of Rio, Niterói, Petrópolis and Nova Iguaçu. Flamengo made it to the final round but lost to América. The cup that year went to Fluminense, so the club were on a bad run of form. The rules for the 1936 edition were simple: clubs had several stages of knockout matches, with the winners advancing and the losers going to a supplementary bracket. In the winners' round, two clubs would advance, and two from the losers' bracket would make the final four. All matches were played on a neutral ground at Fluminense, Laranjeiras, América or Bonsucesso.

Leônidas da Silva was trained by former Flamengo player Flávio Costa, and Leônidas was ready to excel in the tournament. In all, 47 teams participated in the Open Tournament kicking off on 29 March, in which Flamengo debuted later, on 7 April against Modesto. The Quintino club, in a neighbourhood where Zico was born later on, had a very similar jersey to Flamengo. It was a red shirt with a black stripe across the chest, but it didn't help. Flamengo won 6-0, as Jarbas scored a hat-trick, Alfredo a brace and Caldeira one.

Leônidas was born in Rio in September 1913, during a time when football was shunned for black players. Ten years later, in 1923, Vasco da Gama won the Rio State

Championship with players of many different backgrounds in class and colour. That turned the tide for clubs to change their ways. Leônidas began his career at local youth club São Cristóvão, before moving to Sírio e Libanez. It was there he came under the tutelage of coach Gentil Cardoso, who developed Leônidas into a goal-a-game striker. When Cardoso moved on to Bonsucesso he took Leôndas with him, where the young attacker scored 23 goals in his season with the club.

In 1933 Peñarol took him to Montevideo and his first shot at the professional game, which was still unavailable in Brazil. His stay was short in Uruguay, but he still scored 11 goals in 16 league matches. He was called home when professionalism became allowed in Brazil, signing for Vasco da Gama and helping them to a Rio State title. However, after the 1934 World Cup, Leônidas moved again, joining Botafogo, where he won another Rio State Championship.

It would not be much longer before Leônidas moved again, this time to Flamengo in 1936. He became one of the first black players at the club. José Bastos Padilha, upon assuming the presidency of Flamengo in 1934, began instituting changes in the club that would make it the country's most popular. Also brought into the club was Brazilian international defender Domingos da Guia, who had spent the last two years in Argentina with Boca Juniors.

Back home, after another losing effort by Brazil in the World Cup of 1938, Leônidas helped the 1939 Flamengo side win the Campeonato Carioca title for the first time in 12 years, by finishing three points clear of Botafogo. Unfortunately, his time in the red and black shirts of Flamengo was coming to an end, as in 1941 he was convicted of forgery and attempting to avoid a military call-up. For that he was given an eight-month prison sentence, after which he would never play for the club again, moving to São Paulo where he played until 1950, aged 37.

Flamengo's second match of the Open Tournament was on 29 April 1936 against Villa Joppert, an amateur side from the Bonsucesso neighbourhood. This was an outright rout, as Flamengo won 9-2: Alfredo with a hat-trick, and Sa, Engel and Jarbas with braces. In the second half, Villa Joppert were able to sneak two into Yustrich's net. The next match against Bandeirantes from Jacarepaguá was another rout, 8-2, with Alfredo scoring five goals, Caldeira a brace and Engel one. The next match, against Engenho de Dentro, the champions of the sub-league in 1935, was the toughest win, 2-0, with two goals from Jarbas.

As the tournament got closer to the end, the matches got harder. In the fifth round against Bonsucesso, after a goalless first half, Gradim opened the scoring for Bonsucesso before Engel tied the score with a penalty. The match went to a 20-minute overtime, when Alfredo scored the winning goal for Flamengo.

On 16 August, with qualification for the quadrangular round secured, Flamengo played familiar foe Fluminense. Out of Flamengo's group qualifying for the next round were Bonsucesso and América. Flamengo were also able to debut Domingos da Guia and Leônidas for the next round. Like most Fla–Flu matches, this was a back-and-forth match, with Domingos leaving the pitch due to an injury. Sobral opened the scoring for Fluminense after 25 minutes for a 1-0 lead. Jarbas brought Flamengo right back into it not too long after. It was not tied much longer as Hércules put Fluminense up again 15 minutes later. To even up the rivals, Alfredo equalised for Flamengo.

On 29 August, Flamengo faced América, and Léônidas scored a brace with Airton pulling one back for América. This sent them through to the next round, and in the final round they met Fluminense, tying with them 1-1. All Flamengo needed was a victory over Bonsucesso to win the title. It ended up in another draw, after it looked all match like Alfredo's goal on the 23rd-minute mark would confirm them the title. In the 98th minute Alfinete tied the match up.

On 13 September, Flamengo and Fluminense took the field at Laranjeiras for the first game. Just like the matches leading up, it was a tie at 1-1 with goals from Hércules and Jarbas. So a second match took place a week later on the same field. If there was a tie after full time, extra time of two 40-minute periods would define the winner. If, after that, a tie was still on the books, the title would be shared.

The extra time wasn't necessary as Sa waited until the final three minutes of the match to put home the winner. There were 17,000 fans who came to see the win for Flamengo. The Open Tournament was played again the following year, with teams from Minas Gerais, such as Atlético and Siderúrgica. However, it wasn't finished due to politics with Rio de Janeiro football. For Flamengo, it was worth the trouble as it marked the arrival of two great stars. Some would argue that the transformation of the club into a massively followed one took place in the 1930s when popular black idols like Domingos da Guia, Fausto dos Santos and Leônidas da Silva were signed. The matches being broadcast on radio also helped. By the middle of the 20th century, Flamengo already had the biggest fanbase in the city of Rio de Janeiro among the middle and lower classes. The rich people and those with an education followed Fluminense.

So naturally, the Fluminense, América, Botafogo and Vasco fans referred to Flamengo supporters with prejudiced jokes due to social class or skin colour. Some groups of people who would make these jokes would boast of inclusion. At the time, Flamengo had Popeye as their mascot. While it did refer to the roots in rowing, it also showed the idea of resilience which the club were to become so famous for. Argentine cartoonist Lorenzo Molas was the man who came up with the idea for Flamengo to use the character created in the 1920s by American cartoonist Elzie Crisler Segar. Eventually, using Popeye as a mascot wore off because it seemed very strange.

One of the greatest players in Brazilian football history before Pelé turned out for Flamengo. To be fair, he was Zico before Zico, because he was a genius on the ball – Zizinho, or Thomaz Soares da Silva as he was born, in São Gonçalo. Zizinho was always in the headquarters of Carioca, a club which his father was owner and president of, so the sport was in his blood at an early age. Zizinho developed his talent in the football clubs of the city, and soon arrived at Byron. At that time, it was one of the main clubs in Niterói, but it sadly went extinct in 1978.

Eventually, he made his way to Flamengo, and that is where the fun started. As a playmaker he had all the tools: perfect control of the ball, elegance, short dribbling, great vision, a set-piece maven and great runs towards the net. While at Flamengo he was the standard-bearer for elegant midfielders and great in his position. After him came Rubens, Moacir, Adílio and Gérson, all of them playing number 8.

Zizinho was a gritty player who could keep the ball and play a beautiful game. His role models were Oscarino and Clovis, the father of future Flamengo legend Gérson. While at São Cristóvão, he tried to dribble past Afonsinho, who was a Brazilian national team player as well as a police inspector. The veteran did not like the young player showboating him and kicked Zizinho's knees until he had to be helped from the pitch. Flamengo scout Ari Fogaça brought him to the club, but he only got a chance when Léônidas picked up a knock.

In his debut for the junior team against Fluminense, he scored a goal via a bicycle kick very similar to Léônidas's. For a brief period in the 1940s, Flamengo had three of the greatest players in Brazil before Pelé at the same time: Domingos da Guia, Leônidas and Zizinho. In February 1941 Leônidas played his last game for the club, but only left in April of 1942 for São Paulo. In his space, Zizinho got more playing time along with new signings Jayme de Almeida, Pirillo, Vevé and Biguá. This had the makings of a great side along with manager Flávio Costa, who used Zizinho as a right midfielder in the WM formation.

Being so young and so good, Zizinho found himself in the Brazilian national team in January of 1942 for the Sul-Americano in Montevideo. Three other players went along with him: Domingos da Guia, Jayme de Almeida and Pirillo. All of them also helped the club win the Rio title in October, with a 15-match-winning streak. To seal the title, the club tied with Fluminense in the last round to steal it.

The 1943 title was won at more of a canter, with just one defeat in 18 matches, a loss in the fourth round to América. There were massive blowout wins in the run-up to winning the title: 5-1 against Bonsucesso, 6-2 against Vasco and 5-0 at Bangu. Zizinho was there all the time, playing 63 matches and scoring 26 goals. His scoring also set records for the national team: in 1946 he scored four goals against Chile in a 5-1 rout, becoming the first to do as such. It would only be topped against Colombia in 1957 by Flamengo player Evaristo de Macedo. In the Copa América he is still tied for the most goals ever at 17, with Norberto Méndez.

Towards the end of the 40s, as the great team was being broken up, Zizinho stayed consistent. However, he had two serious right-leg breaks and had to miss two straight seasons. He finally returned in April 1947, and players kept away from him so as not to injure him again. Seeing that the players didn't want to touch him, Zizinho left camp to test his leg so that he wasn't afraid. Still, through all of this, he broke his leg again but played on for a bit. Eventually, he took time off to get the leg healed.

After this, Zizinho did come back, but he was used goods for the club and was sold to Bangu. This was a bone of contention with Zizinho, and the club broke up after the shocking 1950 World Cup loss in the final. Legend has it that Flamengo president Dario de Mello Pinto thought that Bangu president Guilherme da Silveirawanted Zizinho, and that it was a joke. Dario proposed a price, and Guilherme wrote a cheque for something huge. As mentioned, the 1950 season was one of the worst in the club's history. Bangu even stomped Flamengo 6-0 in what was called Zizinho's revenge. Zizinho played five years for the club, before moving on to São Paulo where he did win a state title. Eventually, in 1962 at 41, while player-manager at Audax Italiano in Chile, Zizinho hung up his boots. In his career, Zizinho played 328 matches and scored 145 goals.

Some would reckon that Portuguese manager Jorge Jesus evokes the memory of Paraguayan coach Manuel Fleitas Solich, and his impact on the foundation of the club. Cláudio Coutinho built the golden era; Solich built the foundation for Coutinho to come in. In the 1950s and 1960s the club were looking to make a drastic change and compete at the highest level. The main similarity between the two managers was they had different styles from what Brazil were used to seeing.

Flamengo had tried to bring in a foreign manager at the end of the 1930s. They contacted Hungarian Dori Kürschner to update the tactics used. The tactical system en vogue at the time was the WM formation, which generically was 3-2-2-3, where defenders had to spread out to prevent the long ball, midfielders needed the speed and all-round game to cover both zones of the pitch and wingers had to have good crossing ability. The press did not like the new formation, nor when Kürschner moved Fausto dos Santos to the bench. Fausto was suffering from the early symptoms of tuberculosis, which would kill him a few years later.

Flamengo were also experiencing a drought in the Campeonato Carioca; they needed some new eyes on the prize. Flamengo's president Gilberto Cardoso met with Solich, and was so impressed with his work that he named him the new manager. The Paraguayan, in Cardoso's mind, was the person to turn Flamengo into a machine ready to win. Solich's hiring was not a universal decision among the directors. Some wanted to bring in Uruguayan Ondino Viera, though he had a strange passage through Rio, taking in Fluminense, Vasco, Bangu and Botafogo. But he was more of the same – not the change that Solich was. At first, Solich just watched the team as Jayme de Almeida managed the club in a tournament against Botafogo, Boca Juniors and San Lorenzo. Eventually, Solich took over the team, angling them for the top spot in the Rio–São Paulo Tournament.

What Solich was up against in Brazil was a pace of play that was slower, and the star player dictated everything on the pitch. The extra dribble was not allowed, was frowned upon but was not unheard of. In the 1951 Minas Gerais, the champions Vila Nova were led by Martim Francisco, and adopted the 4-2-4 system to benefit the club. In Rio, the system had only been seen upon the arrival of Solich. The man tweaked it even more by playing defender Servílio as what was a midfielder at the time, but in practice in a pair with central defender Pavão.

Solich started out flying, with a 7-2 rout by Flamengo over Bangu in September of 1953. What was so different was that the style was direct, vertical, fast, with the defence covering the zone and the wingers retreating to cover the open spaces. For this type of intensity, the club had to have excellent physical preparation. The extra dribble still wasn't recommended, but could only be used in areas where a player could not pass the ball to a team-mate. Solich also wanted the players always moving; they couldn't stop and stand on the ball because that was easy to defend. He made sure his fundamentals were being taught at all levels of the club. There needed to be heavy physical training, incessant work on fundaments and perfect passes, kicks and headers.

Matt Busby, the Manchester United manager responsible for so many great young players coming through in the 1950s, was very similar to Solich. They weren't shy in promoting young players from the reserves. It was due to two factors: young players took well to orders from first-team members, and they were able to spring a surprise factor for the opposition. Such was the case in Dida's debut against Vasco in October 1954. Benítez and Evaristo, the main strikers, were injured, and their backup Esquerdinha was out too, leaving only the option of the young kid. Solich decided for a local derby to start Dida and Nanny, who had a great rapport. The surprise factor worked as Flamengo won 2-1.

Solich also demanded tactical versatility; it's how he got the nickname Wizard. He could completely change the set-up on the pitch by just moving a player to another zone. This was all before substitutions were allowed. Solich was also willing to sacrifice players, no matter who they were, to win the match or prove his point. He would drop big-time players for matches, because it was his way or the highway. Smoking and drinking were a non-starter for Solich; he wanted his players to stay in great physical shape. No player would consider themselves bigger than the team, though there were great players like Dida, Evaristo and Rubens.

Solich did bring back the great times; the title of 1953 was off the back of 21 wins, four draws and two defeats in 27 matches. The attack poured in 77 goals, but they had a great line-up with García in goal, Marinho and Jordan on the wings, Servílio and Peacock in defence, Dequinha and Rubens in the middle, and Jô, Índio, Benítez and Esquerdinha in the attack.

The titles kept rolling in over the next couple of years. The 1954 Campeonato Carioca was almost identical to the previous year, just with one less win and one more draw. The defence was the key to the title that year, as they let in the least number of goals: 27. However, 1955 went down as a slog for the title. The season started on 7 August 1955 and finally ended on 4 April. The team played 30 matches, with

21 wins, two draws and seven defeats. The club were also lethal in attack, scoring 87 goals.

In the following years, the title wouldn't come back to Flamengo, but they would always be the bridesmaid for the championship. Though they did have an amazing match with Puskás's Honvéd on 19 January 1957 at the Maracanã. Flamengo won over Honvéd 6-4, and it would kick off a series of five friendlies between the two teams, of which each team won two. With all this development of talent, the 1958 World Cup side for Brazil featured many Flamengo players: Rubens, Paulinho, Duca, Índio, Evaristo, Benítez, Esquerdinha, Joel, Moacir, Dida and Zagallo. However, the Brazilian FA did not pick Solich as the manager, claiming he did not have a degree and that he wasn't Brazilian.

Frank left to replace Argentine Luis Carniglia at Real Madrid. While at Madrid he would go by the name Manuel Fleitas, but he would be there only for a year before he returned to Rio in 1962. Among his last acts at Flamengo was finding a very small boy at 18 years old, named Zico. That would be the connection that kick-started the glory years. It did take another ten years for the club to hit their glory era, but when they did, it was because Solich knew where he was going to find talent.

Another one of the great players was Índio – he is one of the top scorers in Flamengo history with 144 goals in 218 matches. Furthermore, he was a stalwart in the three-time champions led by Fleitas Solich in the 1950s. The man with the great header also played in the 1954 World Cup. Índio came to Rio when he was five, after his father died, to live with his older brother. Interest in football took a while for him, but by the time he was in school it was all he thought about. Eventually, he signed to play left-wing for Bangu as a youth.

As little regulation as there still is with the movement of youth in football, it was the Wild West back then. Togo Renan Soares watched Índio play and was so pleased with him that the young player was off to Flamengo the next Monday. For his first two seasons at the club, in 1949 and 1950, he competed with the youth team. Índio's debut finally came on 20 November 1949 in a friendly against Tamoio, which ended in a 3-3 draw. This was a dry spell at the club – Zizinho left and they finished in seventh place in the Campeonato Carioca, the worst year ever at Flamengo. Índio played his first official match in the Rio–São Paulo Tournament on 18 March 1951, taking the place of striker Durval in a 4-2 win over São Paulo.

Índio's coming-out party was Flamengo's trip to Europe. The club played ten matches in Sweden, Denmark, France and Portugal, and they won them all, with Índio scoring six goals in ten matches. In his debut year, Flamengo finished fourth in the championship, and Índio scored seven goals. In 1952 the club would take off, winning the title with a six-point lead over Fluminense, so the good times were rocking.

Índio was in for a treat with the club from here. In 1953 he scored three in a 6-3 win over Botafogo, and again in a 5-2 win over Bonsucesso. He also scored in the 3-1 comeback win over Fluminense. Índio continued with the scoring in friendlies and tournaments on the road. In March, the club won the Buenos Aires Quadrangular Tournament with ties with San Lorenzo (2-2) and Boca Juniors at La Bombonera (1-1, Índio with the goal). The best was yet to come, as Solich would come in as coach.

Índio fitted into Solich's tactics because he was versatile: he could act as a Hungarian-style centre-forward, meaning that he could leave the area for a tackle, opening up space in the opposition defence for one of his other forwards, or just be a disruptive striker. He was short, fast and fought until the last minute, which made him a fan favourite.

In the 1953 Carioca Championship, Índio joined the team in the fourth round, in a 4-0 win over Bonsucesso, Benítez scoring all four goals. Índio played a key role in this, as he opened the holes in the Bonsucesso defence for the attack to go through. He played in a front line of Joel, Rubens, Benítez and Esquerdinha. Índio finished the season with 18 goals, and many of them were against local sides. He could also start a comeback, like one against Olaria in a 3-1 tough turnaround in the final minutes. The goal in the 3-3 draw against Vasco came off his head, tying the match and completing the comeback.

After the World Cup of 1954, Índio came back to Flamengo in great form. In the Rio de Janeiro bi-championship he missed only one of the 27 matches, which helped him become the leading scorer of the team. That included scoring eight goals in the first seven matches. With his attacking partner Evaristo, they kept rallying back from being down to win 3-2. The first time was against South American stalwart Peñarol, who opened up a 2-0 lead through Míguez. The attacking duo started the comeback, just as they would against São Paulo in the Rio–São Paulo Tournament.

Even though Índio was out for a while because of his knee injury, playing 18 of the 30 matches, he still scored 11 goals. In 1956 the club did not get their fourth title, some of it down to losing easy matches early in the season.

Others point to a problem that is still prevalent in the game: exhaustion from continuous first-team play, from exhibitions and the national team.

In a 12-2 victory of São Cristóvão on 27 October at the Maracanã, Índio scored four goals. He followed that up with a dramatic goal in the following 1-0 win against Vasco. He kept trying to get the club back to their title-winning ways, scoring three against Portuguesa, two against Bangu, two against Olaria and one in the Fla–Flu. The 14 goals in nine matches run did get him back into the Seleção for the 1957 South American Championship. Índio played 218 matches, scoring 144 goals.

After those matches, in July 1957 he moved to Corinthians at the tail end of his career in Brazil. In 1959 he moved again to Espanyol in Spain, becoming the first black man to play for the team. Eventually, he hung up his boots for good in 1965, but that would not be the last time a player of his bloodline would be part of Brazilian club football. One of his sons, Frank, using the same nickname as his father, turned out as a right-back for Flamengo in 1986.

Arsenal in North London have always been a top club, and have had their fair share of historic losses. They've also been a destination club for overseas clubs touring for money. On 29 May 1949, Flamengo played Arsenal on the English team's tour of Brazil. Jair da Rosa Pinto showed the British how great a 3-1 win against them could be. In the time after World War Two, civil aviation made it possible for clubs from all around the world to meet each other.

Generally, Swedish clubs like Malmö or Rapid Vienna from Austria came to Brazil. Southampton had come to the shores of Brazil in mid-1948, so Arsenal had to follow them the following season. Arsenal did have better credentials, having just won their sixth league title in 1947/48. The following year they finished fourth. Arsenal came on invitation of Botafogo, and it was on a three-match tour originally. The clubs were Alvinegros, Vasco and either Flamengo or Fluminense, with Trio de Ferro eventually being added. Arsenal's delegation arrived in waves, the first one on 10 May and the second two days later.

Flamengo first needed to get a very good goalkeeper in Paraguay national team and Cerro Porteño's Sinforiano García. Eventually, once García had settled in, he solved the problem of the goalkeeper, as reserve Doly had played in the preseason and let in many goals. The club were also in a steep decline; they turned to a future great basketball coach in Togo Renan Soares Kanela for the following season. As outside of the box as it looked, Kanela had been the football coach a decade before at Botafogo, from 1929 to 1936.

Arsenal's debut in Brazil came at a good time. On 15 May they trashed Fluminense 5-1 in São Januário. However, that would be the last statement win by the Gunners, as they tied with Palmeiras 1-1, and Corinthians 2-0. At this point, there weren't night games in England, and these would only reach the English shores ten years later. Ironically, it was for a friendly, Wolverhampton versus Honvéd, that that would happen. So playing at night was strange for Arsenal, and Vasco won 1-0.

Arsenal were stung by the loss, so Tom Whittaker, their manager, made one change for the Flamengo match, Peter Goring in the place of Ronnie Rooke. García wasn't the only Paraguayan – Bria teamed up with Beto in the middle. Some of the other players in the side were Gringo, Luisinho, Esquerdinha, Durval, Jair da Rosa Pinto and Jajá de Barra Mansa. With all of that, Arsenal started out very well as, after the whistle, Gunners midfielder Macaulay passed the ball on to the right for Logie, who crossed very high to Goring who beat García for a 1-0 lead.

It wasn't too long before the Flamengo fans could start cheering. In the eighth minute Arsenal defender Lionel Smith fouled Durval in the area. Up came Jair da Rosa Pinto for the spot kick – 1-1. The momentum had finally swung to the home team, and the London side did not take too kindly to this. Eight minutes into the second half, Pinto secured the brace at 2-1. Arsenal midfielder Bryan Jones hit goalkeeper García very hard. This, of course, turned the temperature up among the players, and fights kicked off. With the fight on the field, the police showed up five minutes later to remove Jones from the field.

The play calmed down after Jones's removal, and García was able to recover to stop a close-range shot from Lishman. Flamengo could have held on for the win after all this, but Durval sealed it with 35 minutes left in the second half, to make it 3-1. Arsenal still had two more matches on the tour. They drew 2-2 with Botafogo, and lost 1-0 to São Paulo in São Paulo. All was not lost for the Gunners; when they went back to the friendly confines of England, they won the FA Cup, beating Liverpool 2-0 at Wembley.

The Camp Nou is a great place, where South Americans can go and become legends of the sport. Flamengo, like many clubs in South America, have travelled the world to generate more income for their club. In general, South American clubs have suffered for generations, with little to no money in the country or game. It's one of the many reasons for the Santos tours with Pelé in the 60s. Flamengo got to inaugurate the Camp Nou at the end of September 1957.

This was a good side for Flamengo; they had Dida, Henrique and Zagallo, all of whom would wow the Catalan fans in all aspects of the game – technically, tactically and physically, as put down by Paraguayan Fleitas Solich. They did not play Barcelona, unfortunately; they played Burnley, who they thrashed 4-0. Barcelona now and Barcelona then were different.

In the 50s, Barcelona were a growing club, fighting for the Spanish title and the international cups. They were still looking to climb the ladder in the league as a club. Real Madrid and Athletic Bilbao, among others, were bigger clubs at the time. Barcelona's star began to rise when in 1951 they brought into the club László Kubala, a Hungarian from the great international side of the time. The attendances rose substantially to see the great man in action. Their mortal rivals Real Madrid, on the other hand, expanded their stadium to reach a capacity of 120,000. The stadium became the largest in the country, and among the largest in the world.

Barcelona had to do the same, but had a problem. The Les Corts stadium they had been playing in since 1922 had been expanded to its capacity of 60,000. Because of this, President Francesc Miró-Sans looked to build a new stadium in another location to fit their needs. The new stadium was designed by architect Francesc Mitjans, and construction began in March 1954. After more money was put into the construction than first thought plus land problems, the completion didn't come until three years later in September of 1957. The opening was scheduled for 24 September 1957, which was the day of La Mercè, the patron saint of Barcelona. There was a big party in the city, and clubs from all over the world came to participate, including Flamengo and Burnley.

Flamengo were going through a rebuild in 1957. Manuel Fleitas Solich, who had brought in the titles of 1953 and 1955, was still the manager. Big changes had started happening. García wasn't the goalkeeper anymore; Ari had come in. Solich brought in a bunch of kids to add some pace to the group. Joubert became the new right-back as Tomires was phased out, Milton Copolillo took over in central defence and, in attack, Moacir, Henrique and Dida all took their places. If you are seeing some future legends in these names, you are right – Flamengo have always been good at developing talent.

The match in Barcelona wasn't the first time in 1957 that the club had participated in an event to raise funds to build a stadium, or open a stadium. They played in the Morumbi international tournament organised by São Paulo to raise funds for their stadium. In the Maracanã, Flamengo played Dinamo Zagreb, winning 4-1, Portuguese Belenenses, winning 3-1, and drew 1-1 with a combined team of players from Vasco and Santos. Flamengo beat Corinthians 3-1 before São Paulo cancelled the competition due to poor income.

Barcelona offered $8,000 for a match on 25 September in the Spanish city. Flamengo left for Barcelona at 5.30pm on 21 September from Galeão airport on an Air France flight. Once they touched down, the fun began. They were, on the 24th, paraded through the stadium carrying the Brazilian flag while being cheered on by the Catalan fans, all before a match between Barcelona and a combined team from Warsaw.

The next day Flamengo played against Burnley. The Lancashire club were founders of the English League, FA Cup winners in 1914 and league champions in 1921.

Recently, they had come third in 1948, sixth in 1953, and seventh in 1954, 1956 and 1957 in the First Division. So they were a smaller team than Flamengo, but they were good in beating Spanish champions in 1956, Athletic Bilbao, 5-1 in the San Mamés.

The English team were led by midfielders Jimmy Adamson and Jimmy McIlroy – these two would also lead Burnley to a league title in three years' time. Kick-off for the match was at 11am Rio time, and was broadcast on radio through Continental and Mayrink Veiga, together with São Paulo Pan-Americana. Flamengo took the field to a round of applause from the Catalan fans, with Ari in goal, Joubert and Jordan as full-backs, Pavão and Jadir in the centre of the defence, Milton Copolillo, Moacir, Luis Carlos and Zagallo in the midfield, and Dida and Henrique in the attack. The match was played in a hot Spanish summer, but it was not as warm as Flamengo were used to in Rio.

The first Flamengo goal would come in the 23rd minute, as Luis Carlos took a short corner, giving it to Zagallo on the left wing, who crossed it to Dida who headed it past Barcelona goalkeeper Blacklaw. The English couldn't get the ball past the midfield, and Flamengo scored the next goal three minutes later. Jadir advanced the ball to Luis Carlos, who sent it to Moacir, who delivered a short pass to Dida. Dida passed to Zagallo who was racing in, and he hit a thunderous shot into the back of the net for the second. The Catalan supporters roared with appreciation at Flamengo's play.

The match report in *Mundo Deportivo* newspaper showed Fleitas Solich's tactical scheme of the 4-2-4 system. Phrases appeared like 'move with ease', 'change positions' and 'Jadir is a great player to watch'. After half-time, Burnley put pressure on Flamengo's defence to get a goal back, but one of Burnley's defenders, named Winton, passed the ball back to Blacklaw, who wasn't in his goal. It was the dreaded own goal, putting the Rio side up 3-0. It just got worse for Burnley. After 30 minutes of the second half, Henrique put the ball past Blacklaw into the back of the net. That was the final score, 4-0, and because of how well Flamengo were received in Barcelona, the Brazilian giants came back twice more. They played Barcelona in 1962, and won 2-0 with two goals from Dida. In 1968, Flamengo came back again to participate in the Joan Gamper Trophy, beating Athletic Bilbao 1-0 with a bicycle kick by Silva Batuta. However, Flamengo ended up losing in the final to Barcelona 5-4.

Sometimes players from Europe graced the shores of Rio de Janeiro for the simple act of vacationing, and sometimes players came over to play. In September 1966, Flórián Albert, a forward in the Hungarian national team, came on loan from Ferencváros. The Hungarians had been the class of the World Cup that year, and on English soil he tore apart Vicente Feola's Brazilian team. Spirits in Rio were at a high seeing this loan happen, and on 15 January 1967 in a friendly against Vasco, Albert showed his worth. He was also still very well regarded in Europe; at the end of the year he would receive the Golden Ball award from the French magazine *French Football*, as the best player in the world. He was the first holder of the trophy to play for a Brazilian club.

The director of football for Flamengo, a Swede named Gunnar Göransson, brought Albert to Rio. Göransson was a representative in Brazil for Facit, an office supply company. He had fallen in love with the club, and became a member of the board of directors. Albert was not the first European player that Göransson brought to Flamengo;

legendary Soviet goalkeeper Lev Yashin had spent a couple of days in Rio training in mid-1965. Originally, Albert was going to stay with Flamengo but the Hungarian federation limited him to just a month. He could play in friendlies and train with the squad, but that would be it. Flamengo only had to pay accommodation expenses for him and his wife, actress Irén Bársony. Hungary asked him to write down his impressions of the football and training methods in Brazil upon his return.

Albert landed on an Air France plane at Galeão on 7 January, with his wife. On the 9th, he was introduced to the players and staff. While meeting with the press, he talked about playing with Flamengo as he was an admirer of the 1954 squad that had Evaristo, Joel, Jadir, Pavão and Zagallo and was managed by Fleitas Solich. They beat Kinizsi, Ferencváros's name at the time, 5-0. While with Flamengo, Albert spent most of his time taking in training, while barely regarding the social events he was invited to.

Flamengo agreed to play two friendlies with Vasco to show off Albert to the Rio fans, first in Gávea on the 15th, and second on the 19th at the Botafogo stadium of General Severiano. The fandom and the atmosphere were truly cordial, something that rarely can be seen in most matches. On 15 January, the two teams squared off, with referee Arnaldo Cézar Coelho. The Flamengo side, under the management of Armando Renganeschi, still had some good players of the past two seasons: Murilo, Ditão, Jayme, Paulo Henrique, Marco Aurélio, Carlinhos, Pedrinho, Nelsinho, Denis, Osvaldo, Almir-Silva, Albert and César, the brother of Caio.

Vasco had Zizinho, who was their manager at the time. He did have some good players like Oldair, Bianchini,

Ananias, Nado, Adilson and Danilo Menezes. Albert played through the impressive heat, showing great moves and spectacular passes. The crowd was quite impressed seeing this display on the pitch. One of the few social events he took part in during his stay in Rio was the day after the match, a cocktail party at the Hungarian embassy. Albert also took part in a light training session that he was not thought of to participate in. The second match started late at night at 9pm. The most emotional moment of the match came in the 30th minute when Albert came off to a standing ovation. He was off to the airport with his wife, who was waiting for the long trip back to Hungary.

The late 60s were a strange time for the club. Flamengo ended 1969 in a far from glorious way, continuing the trend of the previous three or four forgettable years. A shake-up of the club was needed to push life ahead. Flamengo president André Richer had the perfect man for the job: former Flamengo goalkeeper in the 30s and 40s Dorival Knippel, who went by the nickname Yustrich. The nickname ironically came as a tip of the hat to former Boca Juniors goalkeeper Juan Yustrich, with whom Dorival looked very much alike.

In January of 1970, Dorival replaced Elba de Pádua Lima, or Tim as he went by, as the direct opposite of his predecessor. Tim was not strict at all on player discipline, which could lead to a lack of player production on the pitch. Rumour has it that when Yustrich arrived at the club, he was given an organisation chart from the football department, which he threw out. Yustrich based his style of play on speed and physical preparation. He wanted pressure while marking the opponent, something the Europeans had been doing since the early 60s. Little did they know the 2-1 win over Botafogo on 1 June 1969 in the Campeonato Carioca would be a momentous victory for the club.

So Yustrich and the team that took the pitch on 1 June 1969 had to break with all of this from the past and move on. His predecessor Tim, a striker in the 1930s and 1940s for the Brazilian national team and Fluminense, was very different. Tim was manager at Bangu and in 1964 he won the Rio de Janeiro title with Fluminense. He was one of the greatest strategists in Brazilian football, often explaining things to his players on a button football table.

After the Campeonato Carioca win in 1965 for Flamengo, the club went downhill. They lost the championship the next season under controversial circumstances to Bangu, the aftershocks of which caused the club to have two consecutive bad years following. To stop the slide for 1969, Tim came in from Argentina after taking San Lorenzo to a title in the Metropolitan Tournament. He was also not a manager who dealt with player transfers; he ran the team, not the club. Tim had to worry about how to deal with the three foreigners, when only two could be selected: Argentine goalkeeper Rogelio Domínguez, Uruguayan defender Jorge Manicera and Paraguayan midfielder Francisco Reyes. There was also Garrincha at the end of his career at 35, living more off his legendary status than his present play.

The season started off well in the Carioca, drawing with Bonsucesso 1-1, and beating São Cristóvão 2-0, Madureira 1-0, Bangu 2-0 and Campo Grande 1-0. However, the results did not last: Botafogo beat them 2-0, they lost to Olaria 1-0 and there was a 0-0 draw in the Fla–Flu. By stabilising for the time being, Tim found himself a line-up worth keeping for the season.

In goal, he had ex-Racing and Real Madrid player Domínguez, the full-backs were Murilo and Paulo Henrique, the defenders were Onça and Guilherme, in the middle of the park there were Liminha and Rodrigues Neto, and up top he had Doval, Dionísio, Flo and Arílson. A well-oiled machine, the team won in the last round of the Carioca against Vasco 3-0, with goals from Rodrigues Neto, Liminha and Doval. They won 1-0 against América with a goal from Doval, and then put two past Bonsucesso, Onça and Dionísio the scorers.

With every great run, or side-defining moment, there's a roadblock for Flamengo. Botafogo tended to do that, and they did not know what it was like to lose to Flamengo. They had a two-year winning streak against them in the national tournament, and a four-year one in the Carioca. To add insult to injury, former Flamengo players were succeeding with Botafogo: Zagallo was the coach, and Gérson and Paulo Cézar were part of the side. All of this upset Tim, and he needed to turn the match into a trap for Botafogo. Tim wouldn't have Flo in the attack, as he was out on instruction from the medical department.

Tim went with a line-up of Domínguez, Murilo, Onça, Guilherme, Paulo Henrique, Liminha, Rodrigues, Luís Cláudio Neto, Doval, Dionísio and Arílson. Zagallo met this line-up with Ubirajara, Mota, Moreira, Zé Carlos, Leônidas, Valtencir, Carlos Roberto, Gérson, Rogério, Roberto Miranda, Jairzinho and Paulo Cézar Lima. The referee for the match was Armando Marques, who had a history of controversial decisions against Flamengo.

The instructions came with an unusual change: Luís Cláudio played in the place of Flo, not as a striker but as an attacking right-back. His job was to cheat in on Paulo

Cézar and when he had the ball to fire in long passes into the area from the midfield line. Jairzinho and Roberto were also accounted for. The actual right-back, Murilo, was put in the centre of the defence to mark Jairzinho, while Guilherme was tasked with stopping Roberto Miranda. Onça was moved to the position of libero, which was unique to Brazilian football. On the left side of the defence, Paulo Henrique was there to mark Rogério, and would support when he could fill a gap. In the midfield, Liminha and Rodrigues Neto would form a wall to block Gérson's shots. Neto would follow Carlos Roberto around, and would have his own freedom in support of the attack.

A trident was formed with Doval on the right, while marking Valtencir, Dionísio in the middle and Arílson on the left, going for the overlap. However, he dropped into the middle to see Jairzinho hit the post at the beginning of the match, but after that scare Flamengo were able to have the upper hand. At nine minutes, in Doval received a pass from Luis Cláudio, beat Valtencir and from the bottom of the area crossed the ball to Dionísio, who got past Leônidas. Dionísio hit the target to the left of goalkeeper Ubirajara, who pushed it out for a rebound which found Arílson's foot for the first goal.

Botafogo tried to pull one back, but Flamengo would not let them; Liminha marked out Gérson, Luis Cláudio thwarted Paulo Cézar, Murilo stopped Jairzinho and Guilherme was the same with Roberto. After 23 minutes, Flamengo added to the scoreline through Rodrigues Neto's cross from the left over Valtencir to Doval, who put it in the back of the net.

Botafogo were stunned to see Flamengo playing as well as they were, so Zagallo in the second half moved Paulo

Cézar into the middle. This was to keep him free from Luis Cláudio's marking and to open the space for Valtencir's support. It did not shock Flamengo at all. Luis Cláudio was now marking Valtencir, which gave Doval more space for his counter-attacks. Paulo Cézar was added to the block formed by the Flamengo midfield.

Botafogo were able to get one back through Caju's goal to make it 2-1, with a penalty kick after Jairzinho was knocked down in the area. Suddenly seeing Botafogo come back did not unnerve Flamengo, as they kept their cool. Doval was a constant threat in the attacking half, boxing Botafogo in. In order for Botafogo to get another goal on the board, they needed the ball, which Flamengo were not ready to relinquish. Towards the end of the match Botafogo lost their cool, and goalkeeper Ubirajara grabbed Dionísio by the shorts. Clear penalty, right? Apparently not, as Armando Marques waved it away as the match was ending.

Flamengo were good at playing under adverse conditions, having played in South America their whole lives. Fights, getting kicked and managers getting thrown off the field were generally things that were common in the region. Football matches in Spain were very similar, and the general thought has been for years that Real Madrid get special treatment. On 19 August 1978, Flamengo travelled to Mallorca without Zico and beat Real Madrid. By mid-1978 Flamengo were at an impasse. Zico was emerging as the next Brazilian superstar, but he hadn't raised any great trophies since December of 1974 when he won the Campeonato Carioca.

He came close to lifting a trophy twice, but lost on penalties against Vasco on both occasions – the 1976 Guanabara Cup and the second round of the 1977 Carioca

Championship. However, Zico and right-back Toninho were with the Brazilian national team for the World Cup. Cláudio Coutinho, the manager, was with the national team as well. Flamengo had a bad year in 1978: they were in 16th place among 74 participants.

With all that bad luck out of the way, Joubert, an ex-Flamengo defender in the 50s and 60s, had 28 players throughout the tournament. The problem was quality, and the team was unevenly made from players who weren't really of Flamengo calibre and just not as talented. Coutinho returned after the World Cup to help the club, and Cruzeiro goalkeeper Raul was also brought in to aid the cause.

Before leaving for Spain for the Ciudad de Palma Trophy played in Mallorca, Flamengo beat Atlético Mineiro 2-0. Also on the trip to Spain were midfielder Cleber, striker Marcinho, attackers Tião and Elio Carlos, and midfielders Alberto Leguelé, Olaria and Moisés. Zico, even though the World Cup was over, had suffered a strain so he stayed back. The matches took place on 18 and 19 August, and the clubs competing were Rayo Vallecano, Belgian RDWM or Racing White Daring Molenbeek, Flamengo and Real Madrid. Everyone was actually only waiting for the Flamengo and Real Madrid clash, but they first had to get to that fixture. Flamengo beat Rayo Vallecano 2-1 and Madrid beat Molenbeek 3-2. The final was played the next day at the Luis Sitjar Stadium with a line-up for Flamengo of Raul, Toninho, Júnior, Manguito, Carpegiani, Adílio, Eli Carlos and Cláudio Adão. Three foreign stars were brought in to help during the tournament: Enrique Wolff, Ulrich Stielike and Henning Jensen. Real Madrid were managed at the time by Luis Molowny, and had such great players as goalkeeper Miguel Ángel, defenders Sol, San José and Pirii, and future manager and midfielder Vincente Del Bosque. Referee Jesus Ausocua Sanz would play a big role in the match.

Sanz would make the match about him quickly, because after seven minutes of play Cleber received a throw-in in a good position to score. Sanz blew for a non-existent offside. Two minutes later Tita passed to Toninho, who crossed it in for Cláudio Adão; he put in a shot on Miguel Ángel who pushed it away back into Adão's path for him to score.

There was a mix-up up front on 17 minutes between Adílio and Tita. Madrid, confused by the moment, were bailed out again by Sanz. Jensen tried a bicycle kick and almost hit Manguito's head, sending the ball out of play. It should have been Flamengo's ball, but Sanz wasn't looking at it. Sure enough, Flamengo were able to expand the lead as, on 37 minutes, Cleber came in and put it past Miguel Ángel. On 40 minutes Jensen would make one attack, but he missed the goal.

Flamengo were dominating the match, and the referee wasn't having that. Twelve minutes into the second half, Aguilar was in the penalty area, pushing the ball to Raul's feet, and it was saved. However, Sanz came running in, awarding a penalty for Aguilar and Madrid. Eli Carlos complained to the referee about the penalty and was thrown out of the match. Either way, Aguilar stepped up and scored to make it 2-1.

Flamengo held out. The referee continued to reverse fouls and distribute yellow cards to Flamengo players like he had an agenda. Manguito, Júnior, Tita and Cláudio Adão were all hit with the yellow-card spree, and it continued. On 18 minutes Toninho was hit with a foul and went to the corner as was the expected result. Sanz, however, saw otherwise and pointed for a goal kick, which Toninho complained about. Sure enough, he was thrown out of the match.

In the 27th minute Cleber was fouled, but it wasn't called. So he protested and was given a red card. This sent the Flamengo bench on to the field to protest, and the referee threw out everyone who entered the pitch. That was by the rule book, but not justified. The local fans who were rooting for Real Madrid saw this continued display and began to support Flamengo.

With the referee losing the fans and the players on the field, Flamengo started kicking the ball all over the place. They were also trying to avoid all collisions or anything that could get a card. This was not a safe way to play, and at this point only Raul, Ramirez, Manguito, Nelson, Júnior, Carpegiani, Adílio and Cláudio Adão were left on the field for Flamengo.

Once the final whistle sounded, Flamengo received the trophy and took the Olympic lap in front of 20,000 cheering fans. The referee was booed off the field like Barcelona would have been many times. The main reason for the cynical fouling and one-sided refereeing decisions was that Real Madrid were the favourite club of General Franco and his party. While the General was long dead at this point, having passed in 1975, referees and the crowd were used to the many decades of having to make decisions that favoured Real Madrid.

Before 1981 happened for Flamengo, they set some other great records. This one doesn't go too far back into their history; in fact, it's just a couple of years before. The national league and the state leagues in Brazil have gone through many changes in their names, clubs and so on. This would be the basis for some of the trouble ahead.

South American football isn't without its own history and strange moments. In August of 1978 the state football leagues of Rio de Janeiro and Guanabara merged, which meant the first State Championship. Where the problem came in was that Americano, Goytacaz and Volta Redonda, three clubs from the interior that had played as guests in the two previous Cariocas, were excluded from the 1978 tournament, which would only be played with the 12 clubs of the city of Rio.

At the same time, the Fluminense Championship would take place, bringing together six clubs from the interior to run another tournament. This would contain the first six clubs from the Carioca, and the four best teams from Fluminense would form the ten from the State. Flamengo moved quickly to win the Carioca Championship, ending with a great goal from Rondinelli against Vasco.

A week after Flamengo's win over Vasco, the federation called a meeting to decide what the State Championship would look like from February 1979 onwards. The plan that was agreed on was that everyone would enter the Carioca Championship, with six from the Fluminense Championship. Some of the presidents had a question: if everyone was entered, why did they need to qualify to get in? So the governing body ordered more talks.

Flamengo, while this was being decided, received criticism that they were trying to make the first State Championship count for the 1979 season, not the 1978 season. The reason was that, apparently, they were putting the recently won Rio de Janeiro title at risk. There was good reason for Flamengo to think this: it was odd that a tournament played through 1979 was worth a title from the last year.

What solved the impasse eventually was making a Special Championship, bringing together six clubs from Carioca, Flamengo, Vasco, Fluminense, Botafogo, América and São Cristóvão, and four from the interior, Goytacaz, Americano, Volta Redonda and Fluminense. Then the 18 teams were to be divided into three rounds to be played between May and October, which was unanimously approved. Finally, peace – now on to the tournament.

Vasco were appointed as the favourites to win, but Cláudio Coutinho at Flamengo had other ideas. Coutinho hadn't changed the squad too much for 1979, though Vanderlei Luxemburgo left the team, with Reinaldo and striker Luizinho coming from América. Two players came back from loan spells to help out the side: one was the defensive midfielder Andrade, who could play as far up as striker and came back from Venezuelan football with goalscoring ability, and the other was left-back Júlio César, who came back from América and Remo and was getting better at dribbling and precise crosses.

Flamengo started playing on 8 February; Fluminense and Botafogo had won their first two matches at this point. In that first match Flamengo were short-handed, playing without Toninho, Carpegiani and Zico, but the red and blacks won 2-0 against Volta Redonda at the Maracanã, with goals coming from Cláudio Adão and Reinaldo.

In the second match against a good side in América, Flamengo won 4-0. The first goal by Reinaldo was the first to be announced on the electronic scoreboard of the stadium. Adílio got a goal before a returning Zico scored a brace of two free kicks. Local derbies are always something to look forward to; Fla–Flu is no different from any other. They were playing this time at the Eduardo Guinle Stadium in

Nova Friburgo, and Flamengo won handily 5-1 through two goals from Cláudio Adão, two from Zico and one from Júnior. Spinelli pulled one back for Fluminense. In the next match, against Goytacaz in Campos, Zico scored his 245th goal for the club, passing Dida's mark as the leading scorer in Flamengo history in the 1-0 win.

The next five matches would all be at the Maracanã, and they would all be good games. The first one against Vasco was a 1-1 draw, with Zico scoring a header past Leão, the Vasco goalkeeper. Three days later they beat São Cristóvão 2-0, again through two goals by Zico, as usual. Zico, while being one of the greats, was making this tournament his own showcase.

Another Fla–Flu was in front of them and it was not one of the best matches Flamengo have had. Zico put Flamengo ahead, but Rondinelli deflected a shot from Mario and it went in for an own goal. With the Fla–Flu over with, Cláudio Coutinho put the club through endless friendlies to keep them sharp. But they had another great match against Botafogo, winning 3-0 with goals from Zico, Carpegiani and Luizinho.

That finished off the first round with Flamengo as winners, so they had the task of keeping up the goalscoring in the second round. Their first match was at home against São Cristovão, which they won 6-1, and it was 7-1 in the next home match. Zico scored six goals in this match, becoming the player to score the most in one match in the history of the stadium, a record that still stands today. So far, in ten matches he had 21 goals.

Inbetween two matches, a 1-1 draw with América in which Zico didn't score and a 1-0 victory over Volta Redonda, there was a friendly that would become very famous. Flamengo played Atlético-MG on 6 April, with the revenue from the gates benefiting the victims of the floods of the interior of the country. This was also the match where Pelé adorned the colours of Flamengo. For the first half of the match, more than 140,000 people at the Maracanã were able to see Pelé and Zico on the pitch together. The match ended 5-1 to Flamengo.

Coming back to the real matches, Flamengo went to Campos and beat América 2-1, and then it was the same scoreline against Vasco. They got back to blowing out teams when in the next Fla–Flu, they won 4-0. Flamengo ran to the end to seal the championship, becoming the first club to be undefeated for the 1979 season. They won 13 and drew five of 18 matches. Zico also scored 26 goals in 17 matches.

Chapter 2

Flamengo in 1981

THE STATE leagues in Brazil could fill a book in themselves, but for purposes of space it will only be a chapter. The National Championship had a more detailed configuration, but for the South American, national and worldwide competitions, only the champions and the runners-up were considered. In most other hemispheres, local clubs only have to contest a league, the cups and whatever continental trophy there is in that region. Brazil is different, because it adds another competition. Some of these states have many teams that can actually win the state leagues. Those types of leagues are in the more economically developed states like São Paulo and Rio.

Other states generally have one or two teams that are able to win, so having a national league stops us from comparing teams from smaller states to the large, well-known teams. So the National Championship was very long, lasting from April to December, and it was a remarkable achievement to finish fourth. When cups were involved, like the Brazilian Cup and the National Tournament between the 1950s and 1970s, it was considered a good result being in the finals, even if you didn't win them. With Flamengo, you had to win everything. Fortunately, in 1981 they did.

Brasileiro ends generally in the first week of December, but the clubs don't stop playing there. It's not only a Brazilian thing; the whole continent is like that. There are too many games and the players do not get enough rest. The quality and intensity of the games suffer in key moments. The calendar is out of sync with the rest of the world, making international call-ups for World Cups and Copa Américas disruptive to the teams. Thus, federations pause mid-season to get the international games in. Another issue is that the summer transfer window happens while the Brazilian teams are still playing. Players are taken away in the middle of the league season.

Brazil is a large country, so travel makes the league calendar even worse. For example, if a team travels from São Paulo to Fortaleza, it's about the same distance as from London to Kiev. So to solve this, one would think scrapping or shortening the State Championship might help. A call by traditionalists in football for every federation to align with the FIFA calendar, for both competitions and the transfer windows, would help too.

To highlight the running time for the major club competitions, we can see how long they take. The Brazilian Serie A runs from April to December and is the national league. The State Championship is from January to April, so those two competitions take the whole calendar year up. So realigning the calendar wouldn't help. And that does not account for the cup competitions, where the Brazilian Cup runs from February to October. Add in the continental cups like the Libertadores, which runs the whole year, and the Sulamericana from February to November.

The league system is not without its critics. For the small clubs like Bangu, who have historical significance, there's little chance of them making it to the continental game. Bangu were one of the first clubs to feature black and multiracial players. As mentioned, from January to May, such minor Rio clubs like Madureira, Resende, Macaé, Volta Redonda and Boavista take the limelight in big mismatches against the giants of the region in Flamengo, Fluminense, Vasco da Gama and Botafogo. This scenario is repeated all across Brazil; small clubs don't get the chance to make the National Tournament.

The State Championship reveals a larger crisis in the game: debt. A good majority of the players earn little more than minimum wage, and the soccer calendar is out of sync with the rest of the world. This requires change in the pyramid of Brazilian football. The state federations form the power base of the Brazilian Football Confederation (CBF); they organise the State Championship. So there isn't any personal incentive to change at the federation level, and the CBF won't do anything, so the procession of David versus Goliath continues at no benefit to society. The big clubs have to choose where to send the first team. In 2019, Flamengo's first team was in Qatar for the Club World Cup and there were still state matches at the same time, so they put out an under-20 side against Macaé. The club also failed to reach an agreement with Globo about the broadcast rights, because Flamengo wanted new terms, and more money.

Maybe a change will happen, such as a breakaway to fix the sport somewhat. In England, the biggest clubs broke away from the Football League in 1992 to form the Premier League, which made them very successful and profitable. The CBF, like the country, has had money issues for years. In 1987 a split was in the works. The CBF couldn't cover the costs for running Brazil's domestic leagues. The big clubs formed the 'Clube dos 13', organising their own tournament; this was a way to generate profitable sponsorship deals with Globo and Coca-Cola. Clube dos 13 back-pedalled when their president, Carlos Miguel Aidar, reconciled with CBF's Nabi Abi Chedid. CBF president at the time, Rogério Caboclo, downsized the State Championship to 16 matchdays, mostly a symbolic move at best.

The world was in turmoil from 2019 to 2021 as society was trying to take the shackles off of the status quo, and adapt to the changes of life. The clubs wanted to break away again from the CBF structures to establish new ways to run Serie A, and have greater say in how the game was run. They wanted to show that the overhaul could come into effect as early as 2022, with new proposals, but promotion and relegation would continue. The CBF had been accused of prioritising the national team over the league, using the national team as a globetrotting, money-making unit.

The CBF have been stuck in scandal after scandal, so they had very little to bargain with. Also, by putting the say back into the hands of the clubs, players wouldn't have to leave for Europe so early to make their money. Change is never straightforward, as the CBF's general assembly, made up of 27 state federations, holds voting powers on key decisions. Clubs can only vote to elect the CBF president and vice-president. Also, the general assembly would have to approve the creation of a league body, which would require state federations to vote to give up their own powers to the clubs. Giving the power to the clubs could raise debts; 23 of Brazil's biggest clubs in 2020 hit debts of 1.9 billion US dollars, up 19 per cent from 2019 according to Ernst &

Young,[12] due to revenues being down because of the COVID pandemic.

The architect behind the 1981 success was Cláudio Coutinho, and he had an interesting life. He was a proponent of a technical, offensive style of play, which turned the club into a three-time champion of Rio and they won their first national title at the end of the 1970s. Coutinho was briefly the Brazilian national team manager and manager of North American Soccer League's Los Angeles Aztecs – that's really the grand total of the time he spent in the world focus. Coutinho also died young, so most of his good work was cut short.

Coutinho was born near the Uruguayan border in the city of Dom Pedrito, but moved to Rio when he was four. He supported Flamengo from a young age, and played volleyball at the club, winning three titles between 1951 and 1961. He was also part of the army, and learned five languages. Adding to that, he had a one-year internship at NASA.

When he came back to Brazil, he was given a job on the technical committee of the Brazilian soccer team during the 1970 World Cup in Mexico. This was a great time for the national team, as they were winning World Cups in succession. The 1966 World Cup had gone to England, so Brazil had to set their sights on getting their trophy back. With the grace and technical help of Coutinho, Brazil got their crown back, beating Italy in the final 4-1.

Brazil were never good in Olympic football, so the federation and the government appointed Coutinho head of the football team. He brought with him goalkeeper

---

12 www.sportspromedia.com/news/brazilian-soccer-clubs-2020-revenue-covid-19-brasileiro-flamengo

Carlos, defender Edinho, defensive midfielder Batista, Flamengo's own Júnior and Júlio César. With Coutinho at the helm, Brazil achieved their best result to date, a semi-finals exit.

In September 1976, Flamengo fired manager Carlos Frone. They tried to get former Brazilian national team World Cup-winner Mário Zagallo for a second spell at the club, but he couldn't get out of his contract with Kuwait. Finally, after being turned down by other managers, the federation loaned Coutinho to them for a year. His first match in charge was a 3-0 win in the Maracanã, without Zico (injured) and Luisinho Lemos (suspended). He used a basic 4-3-3, with Jayme as a libero and the midfield closer to the attack.

The great start motivated the club to hire him full-time. As he was on loan before being made permanent, what happened next was out of the ordinary. On 26 February 1977, Osvaldo Brandão stepped down as manager of the Seleção, after a 0-0 draw against Columbia in Bogotá in the opening game of the World Cup qualifiers. The president of the federation, Heleno Nunes, asked Coutinho to manage them for the qualifiers on a temporary basis. So he was loaned back for the time being, while keeping his post with Flamengo. Coutinho managed Flamengo through the 1977 Carioca Championship. Vasco proved to be an unstoppable force and beat them a number of times. At that point, Coutinho left Flamengo to just concentrate on the national team. Joubert, a former Flamengo player, took charge of the club in 1978.

Coutinho was vilified by the press, at least in São Paulo, because he was trying to change the tactics that had made the national team so great. Brazil started out badly in the

1978 World Cup against Argentina and then came into form against Poland to win 3-1. Eventually, the Seleção made it to the third-place game against Italy, winning 2-1. This did a lot of damage to Coutinho's reputation, so after the World Cup he came back to Flamengo to try to repair his image.

Since he had a background in athletics, he developed his tactics around other sports. Like with boxing, he wanted his team to pressure the opponent from the beginning and try to define the match as much as possible. Basketball was also part of it, because of the way the ball was returned to the defence to set up the break. It was necessary to have a complete mastery of the fundamentals. Basketball also showed the team how to slow down and work the ball to the open man.

Coutinho preached the fundamentals of football, and that they had to practise them every day since they would use them when in possession of the ball. They would have to put in passes, kicks, headers, ball control and creativity. Coutinho also continued with the Seleção in 1979 and regenerated the side with new players: Júnior, Falcão, Sócrates and Elder. This new edition beat Paraguay and Uruguay in friendlies before the Copa América, which they didn't win, and Coutinho left the national team for good.

Eventually, he left Flamengo and plied his trade throughout the world, stopping in America with the Los Angeles Aztecs and Al Hilal in Saudi Arabia. At the end of November of 1981, Coutinho watched the Flamengo side after they had won the Libertadores; he predicted that they would win the world title. Unfortunately, he never saw that, as on the morning of 27 November he went underwater fishing and drowned at the age of 42. The nation was in shock after his death.

To achieve the greatness of 1981, Flamengo had to win the league in 1980. That came down to playing Atlético Mineiro, who had strengthened themselves ahead of the 1980 season. They brought in Éder, Palhinha and Chicão to boost their attack. The series of matches was moved around because of a flood in Minas Gerais. Then there was a friendly match on 6 April 1979 where Pelé played in the Flamengo jersey.

Flamengo and Atlético arrived at the match with very similar records; Atlético had one more victory (14 to 13), and Flamengo had one less defeat. Both had scored 43 goals, but Mineiro had the better goals-against average.

Flamengo had home advantage for the title decider at the Maracanã. This was due to the fact that it was down to results obtained from the third group stage on, and in this final stage they had nine points compared with Atlético Mineiro's seven. All the fun kicked off in the second match. At the Maracanã the attendance was 154,355, which was the largest audience in the history of Brasileirão. In the first two minutes of the match, Tita received a yellow card for a foul on Jorge Valencia.

On seven minutes in, Flamengo strung together a great sequence for a goal. Osmar took off with the ball past the Atlético midfield and threaded it into Andrade; he passed it to Zico, who put a pass into Nunes. There, the goalkeeper João Leite rushed forward to block early, but Nunes tucked the ball back into the net for 1-0. Flamengo weren't in the lead that much longer, as Cerezo passed the ball into Reinaldo from the left side and he fired a shot so fierce that it could be considered a lightning strike.

Zico, being the best player in South America, maybe the world at the time, was always on the receiving end of tackles. This match was no different. Seventeen minutes into the second half, Chicão tackled Zico so hard that it could have broken his leg. Zico got back to his feet, only to get knocked down again by Cerezo, who got a yellow card. Right before half-time, Zico put the ball in the back of the net for a 2-2 scoreline.

The play in the second half was free-flowing, with lots of tackles. Most of the play seemed to be going Flamengo's way. Reinaldo, ever present for Atlético Mineiro, scored, putting Atletico up 3-2 after 21 minutes of the half. Towards the end of the match, Adílio passed to Toninho on the right, over Zico's head, which missed the goal. Coutinho wanted the win, not to play for extra time. Constant offensive pushes were showing the intent for the win. Flamengo supporters were on the edge of their seats. The rough play didn't stop, as punches were thrown and the ball was thrown at players; Flamengo wanted the match to end because of all this. Nunes, who always seemed to pop up at the best times for history-making goals, won the title for Flamengo 37 minutes into the second half.

This was the start of three titles in four years for Flamengo. The rise to the top of the world had many possible starting points: the arrival of Cláudio Coutinho, Rondinelli's goal against Vasco or the first national title. Those are all well-known points, but a 5-0 win over Napoli in Italy was a team-building moment, knowing that they could beat clubs outside of South America.

Zico, being as talented as he was, was in the eye of European clubs. AC Milan at the time pushed very hard for Zico to come over. They twice had their vice-president Gianni Rivera and shareholder Felice Colombo in Rio to complete the deal. However, by the end of May the suspense was put to rest, as Flamengo said, 'Zico is non-negotiable.'

Shirt sponsorships were still in their infancy and prohibited in Brazil. One source of income was participating in friendlies and tournaments abroad for a big purse. A mid-year opportunity came knocking on Flamengo's door, when they were invited by Antonio Rosellini, an agent, to Italy. Rosellini was known for taking Brazilian clubs and players to the country. They were to be the first team outside of Europe to take part in the three-year-old tournament, called the Sport Sud International Tournament. It took place in the San Paolo Stadium, Naples, with Avellino, Napoli and Flamengo taking part. The fourth team to join the tournament took a while to confirm, but it became Linfield of Northern Ireland. Napoli had won the first tournament in 1979, beating Bayern Munich, but lost the second one to AZ.

The first two matches of the tournament were played on 12 and 14 June, but Flamengo first had to finish off some state matches. Once they finally set off late in the afternoon of 9 June, they left behind Raul with a dislocated hand and Tita with muscle problems. The line-up that got to play in the tournament was Cantarele in goal, Rondinelli and Marinho in defence, Júnior and Andrade as the wing-backs, Adílio and Zico in the midfield, and Chiquinho, Tita, Nunes and Baroninho up front.

The first match was against Avellino, who had their fair share of Brazilian players in their ranks. They were managed by ex-Botafogo striker Luís Vinícius, and had ex-Santos striker Juary, who was out due to a serious injury he picked up against Inter in January. The other standouts were goalkeeper Stefano Tacconi and midfielder Beniamino

Vignola. Avellino used one striker up top to negate Flamengo's great play and to counter-attack. Flamengo would have none of that as they controlled the match. Adílio put the ball in the back of the net to go ahead in the first half. Then Baroninho scored a brace to give Flamengo a 3-0 lead going in at half-time.

Flamengo were proving to be too much for Avellino. Zico scored the fourth in the final minutes; Leandro made it five two minutes later. Avellino finally got a goal from a header from Giuseppe Massa to make it 5-1. This put Flamengo into the final against Napoli, who had thrashed Linfield 4-0. The prospect of a Napoli and Flamengo final was mouthwatering.

Napoli were a great side in an excellent 1980/81 season. They were led by Ruud Krol, and were close to winning the title. In fact, they went top in the fifth round of the Serie A season when they won 4-0 over Falcão's Roma. Napoli also had an unbeaten streak of 16 matches, conceding five goals, all from Luciano Castellini, who was also a champion with Torino in 1976. However, Napoli finished third after stumbling down the home straight and losing to Perugia.

Any way you describe it, this match was going to be a great one. Andrade got the match off to a flying start with a goal after 11 minutes. Sure enough, four minutes later Adílio hit the crossbar, followed by Zico catching the rebound, only to hit the post, then Baroninho sent the ball out of bounds with his shot. To add insult to injury, a play between Júnior and Baroninho resulted in another missed shot, with the ball going out of play. With all this build-up, a goal had to come. Sure enough, Chiquinho was fouled by Luciano Marangon, getting a free kick on the right side of the field. Chiquinho sent the ball into the area over Zico, but Júnior was hacked down going for the ball by Giuseppe Damiani. Zico stepped up and put the ball in the back of the net for a 2-0 lead.

Napoli's best chance was on 37 minutes: Enrico Nicolini passed to Gaetano Musella, who sent it on to Claudio Pellegrini; he fired the ball off the crossbar into the net. Zico then got back down the field and scored his second of the match, and though some records don't seem to exist, he then got a hat-trick in the match on Italian soil. What we do know is that Nunes also got a goal to round it off 5-0.

The achievement of the match wasn't the trophy but the money and the prestige to Flamengo. It showed the great potential of the club. The midfield was solidified by Andrade, Adílio and Zico. Zico made strong free kicks useful in the Libertadores. It also showed, though Napoli went in for Maradona eventually, bringing him in from Barcelona, that Zico was miles ahead of the Argentine bad boy. And we were still years off the brawl in the Copa del Rey against Atletico Bilbao when Maradona became a bad boy.

Getting into what actually happened for Flamengo in 1981, *The Football Pink*'s founder Mark Godfrey[13] said the Flamengo team were littered with exceptional players, some of whom would be part of the fabled Brazil squad that would gloriously fail at the 1982 World Cup in Spain. There were Leandro, an attacking right-full-back, Júnior, a left-winger, and the crown jewel of the side, Zico. Many considered Zico the world's best player in the late 70s and early 80s.

---

13 www.worldsoccer.com/blogs/when-flamengo-and-zico-ruled-the-world-341585?fbclid=IwAR1eTpUXVnBHzroV7ItdN-r80cJdhO-htc8R7SEX2hPh86D8vmzk0Ddq4w8

He was held in such regard and labelled 'White Pelé'. He was so good that he was given the captaincy of both club and country.

There are many parts to the Brazilian league system, and for the 1981 campaign, Flamengo would have heavy fixture congestion. Not only did Flamengo have to defend their national title from the year before, they also had the Campeonato Carioca domestically. In addition, there was the Copa Libertadores, which had eluded them so far.

The season kicked off in January, with teams joining the National Championship by being put into groups. These groups were created under a new format where teams were placed based on their finishing places in the regional competitions from the previous year. Flamengo progressed through Group D, as runners-up, into the second phase. The quarter-final was against Botafogo, in a two-legged knockout. Unfortunately, Botafogo took them out 3-1 on aggregate so, by mid-April 1981, Flamengo had one competition less to worry about.

Next up for Flamengo was winning back the Campeonato Carioca, which had eluded their grasp since 1979. Determining the champions of Rio had three rounds to it: Taça Guanabara, where the big four, Flamengo, Botafogo, Fluminense and Vasco da Gama, were seeded/ drawn into groups with other participants, Taça Rio, and then a two-legged final where the winners of the first two rounds competed to be crowned the tournament's overall champion. If there was a same winner for both of the first two rounds, then they just crowned one champion without the final.

By July, Flamengo had won the Taça Guanabara, highlighted by a 7-0 thrashing of Americano at the

Maracanã. Having won that initial part and guaranteed their participation in the final play-off, Flamengo could take it easier in the Taça Rio in the latter part of the season. Now, the group phase of the Copa Libertadores was just kicking off after Guanabara was won. The first group stage in the Libertadores was tough for Flamengo as it contained Atlético Mineiro, Cerro Porteño and Olimpia Asunción in Group 3.

Zico and Nunes played their normal best in the competition. Each scored two goals in a 5-2 win over Cerro Porteño, there were two more for Nunes in two 2-2 draws with Atlético Mineiro, and Zico hit a hat-trick in the return fixture at Cerro Porteño. After two victories, four draws and no defeats each between Flamengo and Atlético Mineiro, a match to decide who filled the winner and runner-up spots for the second round had to be played. This was because goal difference wasn't taken into consideration.

The match was played at a neutral venue in Serra Dourada stadium in Goiânia, but it was abandoned after 37 minutes as referee José Roberto Wright sent off five Mineiro players for violence, intimidation and gamesmanship. As is the norm in South America, the police and football officials had to storm the field to quieten the crowd during the melee. Wright walked off the field, giving the game to Flamengo.

The round-robin second stage was taken at a canter's pace for Flamengo. They breezed past Jorge Wilstermann and Deportivo Cali in each of the two-legged matches. The usual suspects were found on the scoresheet: Zico was in his usual goalscoring form, and Nunes and Adílio also helped Flamengo advance to the Copa Libertadores with a 100 per cent record.

The Copa Libertadores is the Champions League of South America, and it was going into its second decade of existence. As World Football Index's Jerry Mancini said,[14] 'The Copa Libertadores de America dates back to 1896. It was named in honor of the soldier presidents who led the fight for independence in various South American countries.' The first tournament was in 1960 and seven teams competed. Peñarol, with the great Alberto Spencer, were the first champions, beating Olimpia. Peñarol went back the next year and won the whole thing again.

In the next decade, the 1970s, Argentine clubs were dominant in the Libertadores – from 1972 to 1975, Independiente won four consecutive titles. That record hasn't been matched to date, even with the runs of titles some clubs have gone on. Independiente are still the most successful club in Copa Libertadores history. To finish off the 70s, Boca Juniors, another Argentine club, won two straight titles in 1977 and 1978, and tried to make it three in a row in 1979 but lost to Olimpia.

The final wasn't against a traditional continental power. In fact, it was against a club that was four years old. Cobreloa, from a desert mining city in Chile, were formed in 1977. Andreas Campomar in *Golazo!*[15] said, 'The title challenge had come down to the penultimate match of the season. With Cobreloa and Universidad de Chile level on points, the latter, having led by one goal to nil against Lotaedc Schwager, conceded a penalty in the ninetieth minute.' The club won its last two matches of the year to win the title. They were also financed by División Chuquicamata de Codelco, a state-owned mining company which put many pesos behind acquiring talent.

---

14 https://worldfootballindex.com/2019/11/from-penarol-to-river-a-concise-copa-libertadores-history/

15 *Golazo!* – Andreas Campomar, pp 364–65.

The area can be described as '*Calama – Tierra de sol y cobre*', the land of sun and copper.[16] The city is west of the Andes Mountains in northern Chile in the driest part of the desert on Earth. Because of this, the interior doesn't lend itself to massive migration. Since Spanish colonisation, the capital of El Loa province has stayed small, but is an important town for trade and mail routes.

One particular mineral that's abundant in this harsh climate is copper. This alone helped the area grow and sustain its inhabitants through the ages. Its economic value is immense to those around and shaped by society's exploitation of it for the many things it can be used for. This is being brought up for the purpose of explaining that, for many years, 44 to be exact, since the founding of the Chilean Primera División in 1933, Calama were without a major club. It didn't even have a club to compete against the Santiago-based clubs of Colo-Colo, Universidad de Chile and Universidad Católica. When Cobreloa came in in 1977, that all changed. There's an interesting point behind the name: it's an amalgamation of Cobre, the Spanish word for copper, and Loa, after the region and the longest river in Chile that flows close to Calama.

After a full year of campaigning with the phrase 'now or never', Cobreloa's application to join the professional leagues was unanimously approved by the league. On 7 January 1977, police chief Francisco Nuñez Venegas announced that the club had been admitted into the professional leagues, to the excitement of the citizens who flooded the streets to celebrate the announcement. They were nicknamed the

---

16 https://footballpink.net/from-copper-to-the-copa-the-meteoric-rise-of-cobreloa/

'*zorros del desierto*' – the desert foxes. By the time the club made it to the top division, they became great and it only took them a year to figure out how to win the league.

As the start of the next decade saw the price of copper skyrocket, Cobreloa's ascent to the top of the Chilean league was put into the hands of Vincente Cantatore. Until this point, he had only worked with Lota Schwager, but he would later have a long coaching career in both Chile and Spain. His debut year? Just four league defeats en route to their first Chilean league title.

Next, they had to conquer the Copa Libertadores, and their previous attempts to get in had ended in the qualifying play-offs. This time, with the title win they qualified and were placed into Group 5 with Chilean club Universidad de Chile, Sporting Cristal and Atlético Torino. Cobreloa breezed through the group stages into the round-robin phase. There, they met with far tougher opponents – Uruguayan giants Nacional and Libertadores veterans Peñarol, who were also the holders.

Sure enough, Cobreloa made their way past both clubs, earning their place in the final against Flamengo. The first leg of the final was on 13 November 1981 in the Maracanã Stadium. Around 94,000 fans of Flamengo were there to greet the Chilean champions. Here are some facts about the Libertadores Final.[17] The players in the first leg were Mozer, Raul, Marinho, Nel Dias, Andrade, Júnior, Tita, Leandro, Nunes, Zico and Adílio, who had a bandage on his forehead after a stone hit him in the head during the Santiago game. The home side saw Zico put them up 2-0 at half-time, and it looked like this was Flamengo's Libertadores to lose. That

17 https://flamengoalternativo.wordpress.com/tag/libertadores/

was all put on hold for a bit when Víctor Merello blasted home a penalty to give Cantatore's men some hope for the return leg at the national stadium in Santiago, Chile.

This time, a week later, in front of another typical, massive South American crowd, nerves of both sides were frayed watching the clock tick down to Flamengo's aggregate victory. However, with less than five minutes remaining, Merello once again came up as the hero. He stepped up to take a free kick 25 yards from goal, and guided by a slight deflection and to the delight of the majority of the 60,000+ supporters in the stands saw the ball glide into the top corner of the net past Flamengo keeper Raul to draw Cobreloa level. After that there wasn't extra time, but instead a winner-takes-all decider in Montevideo just three days later.

Zico was up to his normal goalscoring magic, scoring two, one in the first half after confusing the defence, and another late in the match to break the tie at 2-1. Like most finals in South America, the rough and tumble part of the game got out of hand. Brawls were part of the game during this era, and five players were thrown out of this match: Flamengo's Andrade and Anselmo, and Cobreloa's Eduardo Jiménez, skipper Mario Soto and Armando Alarcón. Alarcón scored the first goal in Cobreloa's first game. Anselmo was escorted from the field by the police for his part in the brawl, ironically just three minutes after coming on as a substitute.

Flamengo now had a Copa Libertadores to their name, but after looking over this, there are many misconceptions about the tournament at the time used to discredit the win. One could think that this edition of the Copa Libertadores looked to be very easy for Flamengo. That could be to do with the rules of the time – each country had the right to two representatives. In Brazil's case, there was only one national tournament, so the champions and the second-place finisher of the Brasileiro participated. In the first phase, the 20 clubs were divided into five groups of four teams each. One team from each group qualified for the semi-finals. If there was a tie, an extra game was played. Once in the semi-finals, the group was joined by the current Libertadores winner.

The semi-finals contained Flamengo, Nacional, Peñarol, Cobreloa, Deportivo Cali and Jorge Wilstermann. It would have been better for Flamengo to face the Uruguayan giants due to proximity. But they were drawn into a group with Deportivo Cali and Jorge Wilstermann.

Deportivo Cali of Columbia had a good history in the competition; they were runners-up in 1978 to Boca Juniors, and in ten years they were undefeated at home in the competition. They also, in this edition, took out River Plate in Buenos Aires. So in fact, Flamengo didn't face the Argentines but the executioner, as one could say of the Columbian club. The two-legged series against Deportivo Cali resulted in a 1-0 win in Colombia and a 3-0 win in the Maracanã.

Wilstermann boasted the altitude of Cochabamba, 2,560 metres above sea level, and the fact they were the first Bolivian club to make it to the second stage of the Libertadores. They did have an old rival of Flamengo in Jairzinho. He left before the first match between the two, but for Botafogo, and lost with his new club 6-0 in the Campeonato Carioca. Flamengo beat Wilstermann 2-1 in Bolivia and 4-1 back at the Maracanã without Raul, Leandro, Mozer and Zico.

Flamengo's title and the following win in the Intercontinental Cup changed the paradigm of Brazilian football. They had lived off of the episodic conquests of the Libertadores with Santos and Cruzeiro. Now they could live with aspirations of the South American trophy and the World Cup in Tokyo. What Flamengo showed were stars in every position, and an outstanding number 10, and they could set a goal and know the hard work and preparation to achieve it.

We should focus on the groups and run-up to the Copa Libertadores.[18] Flamengo are Brazil's most popular club with a reported 39 million supporters nationally and millions more worldwide. The time period between 1980 and 1983 was what made the club the global force that it is today. Until this point, they had never won a domestic or continental top-level honour. With some of the most important and popular footballers of all time, that changed.

In Flamengo's first group encounter, they drew with fellow Brazilian side Atlético Mineiro 2-2, before winning the next match against Cerro Porteño, with Zico and Nunes each scoring a brace. That momentum stopped as they drew the next three of their four remaining group games. The only win was a return match against Cerro Porteño as Zico scored a hat-trick. The group ended with the two Brazilian clubs tied at the top on eight points. Flamengo did finish top due to their superior goal difference. Even with all of that, there had to be a play-off to determine who would win the group.

Nothing is straightforward when it comes to matches in South America, and Flamengo's progression to the next round was a circus. They progressed as referee José Roberto Wright had called off the match. Atlético had five players

---

18 https://boxtoboxfootball.uk/flamengo-ruled-world/

thrown off inside 40 minutes, so Wright had to abandon the match because of a lack of sportsmanship, and violence. This was a lucky escape for the club.

In most of the football-playing world, continental progress is prioritised over the league, such was the case with Flamengo in 1981. They were not at their best in the Brasileiro; they showed fatigue in their play and weren't as dominant in the domestic league as they were in the continental competitions. After making it through the two round-robin group stages in Brazil, they dispatched Bahia in the round of 16 but lost to Botafogo in the quarters.

This stacked line-up was unstoppable mostly because of the attacking talent, but that leaves out the play of the defence. Led by Carlos Mozer and Marinho in the centre, they were flanked by Leandro and Júnior as full-backs. The full-backs revolutionised offensive defenders for decades to come. Leandro, the right-back, was quality in both halves of the pitch, and a proven scorer. Júnior, the left-back, is one of the most iconic Brazilian footballers. He could use both feet equally, play in the midfield and had a great eye for goal.

There was a sad note among the ranks of Flamengo with the death of ex-manager Cláudio Coutinho. This took place just a week before Flamengo took on Vasco da Gama in the Rio State Final. Flamengo, spurred on by emotion, regained the Campeonato Carioca after a 2-1 win, which was dedicated to their former leader. Júnior presented a match-worn shirt to Coutinho's son.

Not all matches were wins for Flamengo.[19] In fact, local rivals Botafogo took them out in the quarter-finals of the

---

19 www.vavel.com/br/futebol/2017/08/16/botafogo/817585-relembra-e-viver-subestimado-botafogo-elimina-maquina-do-flamengo-em-1981

Brazilian Championship in 1981. At this time, the match lasted 180 minutes, two games of 90 minutes each. The first leg had little emotion and no scoring. All the fireworks both on and off the field came in the second leg. This was attended by 135,000 people at the Maracanã. Just after the kick-off, Zico opened the scoring, and kept the Botafogo fans on their toes until near the end of the first half. On 44 minutes, Botafogo's Mendonça equalised with a great header.

The second half was just as tense as the first. Jérson put Botafogo ahead and stunned the crowd in the Maracanã. This wasn't the last goal as Mendonça went on a great run past Júnior and put the ball past Raul, the Flamengo goalkeeper. That was the winning goal that put Flamengo out. The win also stopped a five-game losing streak in the Brazilian Championship against Flamengo for Botafogo. This didn't start another winning streak as Botafogo went out in the next round.

As deep a rivalry as Fla–Flu is, Flamengo have history with another club in the Rio State: Botafogo. Among Flamengo supporters, the 6-0 rout over them on an overcast Sunday afternoon on 6 November 1981 is well known. It was retaliation for the 15 November 1972 Botafogo win for the Brazilian Championship with the same score. Flamengo had two other chances to overturn the score, the first being on 19 July 1975 when Flamengo scored three in 13 minutes. However, they started to slow down and it made the crowd very angry. They were so angry that at the end, after the fourth goal was scored, the fans cursed out the players and broke into two of their cars outside the Maracanã.

The second time came on 18 March 1979 when Flamengo scored three in 40 minutes. However, in the second half they played just to keep the score, not to add more. This time there wasn't a riot or problems with players' cars, as the majority of the 128,106 fans left the stadium frustrated. They finally got revenge in the autumn of 1981. By this time, the crowd was half the size at 69,051, as it had been raining for a while in Rio. Nunes made it 1-0 on seven minutes, Zico 2-0 on 27 minutes, Lico 3-0 on 33 minutes and Adílio 4-0 on 40 minutes. So 6-0 was possible at this point, as it wasn't even half-time and Flamengo were more than halfway there. Of course, the crowd wanted more and chanted 'we want six'.

The anxiety of wanting six reached a new high in the first half hour of the second half when Adílio was taken down in the area by Rocha, thus being awarded a penalty. Zico put it home for the fifth goal. Now the anxiety had reached a very high level as they saw the team move on with the match. Finally, in the 42nd minute of the half Andrade took off for goal and put the ball past Paulo Sérgio for the 6-0 win.

It's also worth noting that there were other side matches and tournaments that Flamengo took part in. One was a testimonial for Paulo César Carpegiani, who retired to become the manager on 15 September, against Argentine giants Boca Juniors. The other was the Naples International Tournament from 12 to 14 June. The tournament in Naples showed how powerful Flamengo could be, as they won 5-1 over Avellino, a mid-table Serie A side at the time. Against a more well-known side, they beat Napoli 5-0 at a very crowded San Paolo Stadium.

During the early autumn, Flamengo were able to schedule a testimonial for Paulo César Carpegiani against Argentine giants Boca Juniors. The talk around this match would be the match-up between Zico and the emerging talent of Diego Maradona. They had never been seen on the same pitch together. Diego had made noise as a prolific goalscorer for Argentinos Juniors in the late 70s. February 1981 saw Argentinos Juniors loan Diego Maradona to Boca Juniors for a reported five million dollars.[20] Zico scored both goals in the 2-0 win, and in the second half Maradona had a scoring chance late in the game.

Flamengo were more than just Zico. There was talent everywhere, which made them the machine that they were. Some did come through the academy like Zico, and some had to obviously be brought in to fill spaces. In order to get the well-oiled machine that they became, they had to chop and change.

A couple more great players for the side were central midfielder Adílio and striker Nunes. Adílio won almost everything during the Golden Age at the club, which he was around for from 1975 to 1987. Adílio also sits third on the list of most appearances for the club and, more importantly, scored one of the goals in the Intercontinental Cup against Liverpool in 1981. He was capped twice for Brazil between 1979 and 1982. Nunes was a star striker for the side, popping up with a goal here and there. He actually started his career with Flamengo but never got into the first team and left, becoming a star for Santa Cruz, Fluminense and CF Monterrey. Nunes returned in 1980 to Flamengo and became one of the most important players of the generation. Despite all of that, he was only capped six times for the Brazilian national team.

---

20 Boca Juniors: *A History and Appreciation of Buenos Aires' Most Successful Futbol Team* – Stephen Brandt

We can't go much further without mentioning Leovegildo Lins da Gama Júnior, better known as Júnior. He was one of the best right-backs Brazil have ever produced, even playing in the midfield too. He was a multipurpose player, ambidextrous and showed lots of technique, earning him an invite to the Flamengo academy. Once he got his shot at the pro team, he was put in another position: right-back.

This is when his ascent to be one of the greats started. Júnior scored his first goal in the 1974 State Championship to win the title. In 1976 he would become more versatile as he started at left-back. He was a very reliable player, and would miss very few matches due to injuries. He would play 876 matches, with 508 wins, 212 draws and 156 losses. And he was on the field for all of those matches.

Goalkeeper Raul Guilherme Plassmann was convinced by Cláudio Coutinho to be the voice of experience for a young Flamengo side in 1978 when he was signed from Cruzeiro. Raul became an idol at Flamengo pretty quickly. He showed the emotional balance and command of the defence that great goalkeepers needed to have. Raul was known for wearing his yellow shirt because it had a mesmerising power over attackers, as they kicked the ball in the direction in which he was positioned. The shirt colour was adopted by other goalkeepers over the years at the club, all the way up until the 2018/19 season when Júlio César retired with it.

Raul was a prominent goalkeeper with two Libertadores titles, in 1976 with Cruzeiro and in 1981 with Flamengo. He only had a short spell with the Brazilian national team and was capped 17 times between 1975 and 1980. He was thought of for the 1982 World Cup by Telê Santana but had to miss out due to an injury. In 1983 Raul retired at Flamengo after the Fla–Flu match.

The defenders Marinho and Mozer were in front of Raul. Marinho started out at Londrina between 1974 and 1979, playing 44 matches for the club. He played briefly on loan at São Paulo in 1977, when they won the Brazilian title. At the end of the 70s he scored six goals for Londrina in 1978, and seven in 1979 in the Brazilian Championship. That along with his overall play is what made Coutinho bring him to Flamengo in 1980. By the time he left in 1984, he had played in 218 matches, achieving 123 wins, 57 draws and 38 losses. While playing with Flamengo he won three Brazilian titles, the Copa Libertadores in 1981 and the Intercontinental Cup. Marinho played only twice for the Brazilian national team.

Mozer was born in Rio, and rose up through the academy to feature with the pro team. He was part of the 1980 under-20 title win with the club. When he finally made it to the pro team, he played 292 games from 1980 to 1987. There were 166 victories, 68 draws and 58 defeats during that stint. He played as a centre-half and scored 21 goals. Mozer was a consistent player at the back for Flamengo, playing 12 of the 13 matches in the Libertadores campaign in 1981 and being on the field for the Intercontinental Cup.

Adílio and Andrade helped link the defence to the attack. Adílio came through the academy, making it to the first team in 1975. In his career he played 617 matches, the third most at Flamengo, which translated into 377 wins, 148 draws and 92 losses. He scored 129 goals for the club. Along with the wins and the goals came titles, medals and glory. He took the number 8 shirt, winning Guanabara Cups in 1978, 1979, 1980 and 1981, State titles in 1978, 1979 and 1981, a Brazilian title in 1980 and the Libertadores in 1981, along with the Intercontinental Cup. Adílio scored one of the goals against the European giants Liverpool in the Intercontinental Cup. For his great career he only played twice for the Brazilian national team, once in 1979 and again in 1982 in a match against Germany at the Maracanã when he assisted Júnior's goal in the victory.

His midfield partner Andrade was one of those players you had to see to behold. He had great technique and could hit long shots with perfection. In his career he played 570 matches, with 332 wins, 139 draws and 99 losses, scoring 29 goals for the club.

Striker Nunes was another one of those great players for the club that kept defences from only focusing on Zico. Nunes came through the youth system but was free to leave for Sergipe, where he started his professional career for Confianca. While there, he became an idol, winning his first two titles in his three years at the club. In 1978, another club in Rio came in for him, this time Fluminense, but he wasn't good there and left for Monterrey.

Finally, in 1980 Nunes came back to his favourite club Flamengo, albeit he was 26 by that time. His arrival helped bring more success because teams couldn't just focus on Zico. Nunes was an all-round player that the supporters loved. While at the club, he scored 99 goals and collected many titles. He made a point of scoring in big matches or finals – just his way of giving back to the club.

Nunes's best year with Flamengo was 1981; in the Brazilian Championship he got 51 goals. For his efforts he got the Silver Ball as the top scorer in the championship. He didn't stop scoring there; in the Libertadores he got six more goals. In the Intercontinental Cup he scored two, as was his normal number of goals.

As we keep looking at the players for the side, next up are Lico and Tita. Lico started his career playing as a striker at América de Joinville in 1970, before being loaned out in 1972 to Grêmio. He returned to Santa Catarina in 1974, playing for clubs like Figueirense, Marcílio Dias, Avaí and Joinville. At Joinville he wore the 10 shirt, winning the bi-championship in 1979/80 and scoring 12 goals. With all of this, he became a legend at the club, but his time there was going to be short. Flamengo coach Cláudio Coutinho took some interest in him. In 1980 he made the move to Rio to play for Flamengo, originally as a backup for Zico. His first game of note was in the revenge match against Botafogo mentioned above. He scored one of the goals, and from then on, he was part of the Flamengo attack. Lico played in two of the three matches in the Libertadores Final, five of the 13 in the Libertadores, and was part of the Intercontinental Cup team too.

Tita, who was born in Rio, started his time at the club in the youth system. He moved up to the first team as a forward in 1977, but had a crowded forward group to contend with, so he was moved out to the right wing. He had great vision and speed but could be defined as a point guard on the pitch. In his number 7 shirt, he played 391 games, with 247 wins, 97 draws and 47 losses. He scored 136 goals, and was on the field during 12 of the 13 matches in the Libertadores of 1981.

Leandro is one of the best right-backs to play the sport, not just in South America, but the world. He came through the youth set-up and made his debut with the first team at the young age of 19. By the time he was done, he had played 415 games. Leandro was so good that he could play many positions, and even as a young man he would play with his non-dominant leg to develop it. During the 1981 Copa Libertadores, he played in 13 of the 14 matches, but was ever present. While at Flamengo he only scored 14 goals; however, they were important.

The great Zico is described by Gary Thacker in *Beautiful Bridesmaids Dressed in Oranje*: 'The magical Zico, perhaps the true heir of Pele, in the No. 10 shirt.' That's a big point to talk about. Zico was called the 'White Pelé', and wearing the 10 shirt, he was able to put great passes in, dictate the play while providing the wonderful football we all expected to see. Like many, Zico was very small and only topped out as an adult at 5ft 8in.

Zico was born in Rio de Janeiro in the Quintino Bocaiuva neighbourhood on 3 March 1953 to a middle-class family who had Portuguese in their blood. He often skipped class to play football at Juventude, a small club in Brazil. It was an unknown club before he showed up. By 1968 it was obvious that Zico was going to progress to the top of the sport, so he secured a trial at America in Brazil. While on trial, he played a match for them, showing some of his amazing skill. Zico caught the eye of a local reporter who suggested to Zico's father, José Antunes Coimbra, a former player himself, to take Zico off to Flamengo. The club almost turned the future great away because he was so small, apparently only 4ft 8in at the time. Even through all of that, Zico played 116 matches in the youth team.

Spain of 1982 was supposed to be the coming-out party for the Brazil team. Pelé's group had been retired; now the next great group was out there. In this World Cup would be the great players of Zico, Paolo Rossi and Diego Maradona.

Zico, at 29, was just off the back of conquering the world in Tokyo. Rossi was serving his ban from the Totonero scandal in 1980 in Buffalo, New York, playing in the Buffalo Stallions[21] indoor team. Because of the ban, he couldn't play for a FIFA-sanctioned team and the Stallions weren't. So on 30 October 1980 at the Aud in a preseason game against the Philadelphia Fever, Rossi scored two goals in the 9-8 win. Paolo only spoke Italian, and forward Pat Ercoli was his translator. Ercoli later in life worked in management with the Rochester Rhinos in America's lower leagues. After the match the players all went out for the night to Mulligan's Brick Bar on Allen Street in Allentown, a local community in Buffalo.

All the big clubs in Europe were keen on getting Zico to come over, like Maradona had just done previously. This was an era where Brazilian players did not immediately go to Europe. Sometimes, this was their choice; sometimes, it was because the Brazilian military government wouldn't allow players to leave. Secretary of State during the Richard Nixon administration, Dr Henry Kissinger, had to negotiate the transfer of Pelé from Santos to New York Cosmos after Pelé had retired. Zico was the chance that Europe could have had at a Pelé-like figure they had missed out on. Zico and Sócrates were two great names, and players that worked directly at odds with each other. Sócrates could work with a slow build-up play that Telê Santana wanted. If one wanted to compare Zico with an English Premier League great, he was very similar to future Chelsea great Gianfranco Zola, the comparison relating to

---

21 www.frontrowsoccer.com/2020/12/12/soccers-italian-stallion-when-world-cup-hero-paolo-rossi-played-with-the-indoor-buffalo-stallions/

how slow they both were. Zola and Zico were so naturally talented that they could score on their own, but their pace would also get them into positions to get the ball to another speedster. Brazil in 1982 ended up becoming like Hungary in 1954 and Holland in 1974; great sides with great talent that didn't win the World Cup.

A year after the great failure of 1982, at 30 years old, Zico left for Serie A. Granted it was a decade after most clubs had wanted him, and the giants of Milan, Turin and Rome stayed away, but he was there. It was a smaller side, Udinese, that finally brought him over. He wasn't the only Brazilian in the team; there was also Edinho, captain of the 1986 Brazil team. Friulani loved Zico from the start, and he stayed for two years with the club. They rushed to the ticket office and bought 27,000 new season tickets, a record up to that point.

In Zico's debut season of 1983/84, he came second place to Michel Platini in goalscoring. In 1985, Zico returned to Flamengo in order to prepare himself for the 1986 World Cup, but his body began to wear out on him, as he kept getting injured. Those injuries forced him to retire by the end of the 80s. Zico also left Italy after being convicted with tax evasion. In 1988 he appealed the tax evasion conviction to the Triste Court, and it was overturned.

By the early 1990s, Zico was in Japan, and was playing again. He is known as the grandfather of the modern game in Japan after he retired once more in 1994. Zico stayed there coaching and in upper management. He even managed the Japanese national team.

Coaching in South America is tough – the fans, the media and the club expect wins. It's a pressure cooker; if you don't win a match, you're gone. The rate of turnover, even after a great season, is pretty high. Just look at your favourite club's history of management and you'll see a bunch of managers come and go. In fact, you might see the same name come and go many different times. During the 1981 season, Flamengo had three different coaches, in a year when they were dominant. Former midfielder for Flamengo, Modesto Bria, started out the year as the manager in his third and last spell in the position. He lasted until 5 April. That's when Dino Sani came in as a coach,[22] and he was one of those former players who played in the 1958 Brazilian team that won the World Cup. He played more than 300 games for São Paulo between 1954 and 1960, and briefly turned out for Boca Juniors. During his coaching career he launched many Brazilian superstars: Falcão, Carpegiani, Claudio and Leandro. As a manager at Flamengo, he presided over 24 matches, gaining 13 wins, eight draws and three losses, with 53 goals for and 29 against.

He was replaced by a former player, Paulo César Carpegiani. Carpegiani started his career at Internacional-RS with Falcão for the club that won the Bi-Champion of Brazil in 1975/76. He came to Flamengo in 1977 and began to win titles as a player. He won the Tri-State Championship in 1978/79 and the Brazilian Championship in 1980. A second major knee injury forced him into retirement; he had had an operation on a meniscus in 1975. Carpegiani took over the Flamengo team in 1981 during the Libertadores campaign, winning both the Libertadores and the Intercontinental Cup.

There are some misconceptions about the Libertadores in 1981 that we should dispel before going any further. The

---

22 https://redacaorubronegra.com/lendas-do-time-de-1981-tecnicos-e-reservas/

great thing with books, articles and the internet is that if you need to find something, it is out there. Gaining information on Flamengo in English is a challenge but the number of resources about the club is great. The Libertadores has snuck into the consciousness of many footballing hipsters. There is a great Portuguese Flamengo blog called *Flamengo Alternativo* that goes deep into many aspects of Flamengo and its history, one of these being the reasons why the Libertadores in 1981 was better than we think.

The first issue to dispel is that this was an easy Libertadores.[23] The rules of the competition at the time were different to now; each country only had two representatives. In the case of Brazil, where there was only one national tournament, the champions and the runners-up participated. One from each group moved on unless there was a tie, and an extra match was played on a neutral ground. In their group, Atlético Mineiro were well known to Flamengo, Olimpia had experience in the Copa Libertadores, having beaten Boca Juniors, and Cerro were a new club, as mentioned. Olimpia and Cerro, however, formed the basis of the Paraguay team that won the Copa América in 1979, not an easy thing to do.

Another misconception brought up is that this wasn't a good era for Argentina. However, River Plate and Rosario Central would say otherwise. River had all the talent: Fillol, Tarantini, Passarella, Alonso, Houseman, Heredia, Ramón Díaz, Ortiz and Kempes. All of these players were in the Argentine World Cup champions team of 1978. Rosario Central didn't have well-known players, but they played

---

23 https://flamengoalternativo.wordpress.com/2011/11/25/mitos-e-fatos-sobre-a-libertadores-de-81/

in a great league. Both clubs were surprisingly eliminated from the tournament in the group stages. Deportivo Cali put one nail in the coffin of River, winning 2-1. People also talk about the Falklands War in terms of players boycotting the Argentine teams. However, the war was a year after this tournament, sothis was not the case.

At this point, the Uruguayan sides Nacional and Peñarol, both hated rivals, were strong contenders in the Libertadores. Peñarol had a very strong history in the competition, winning the first two editions and in 1966. As an aside, Peñarol won the Libertadores in 1982. Deportivo Cali and Jorge Wilstermann weren't pushovers when Flamengo got to the second round. Deportivo Cali had a history in the competition, having finished runners-up to Boca Juniors in 1978. They had also not been defeated at home for ten years in the tournament. A strong résumé but it gets stronger, as they were the ones who finally put River out in Buenos Aires. Flamengo won 1-0 in Colombia and 3-0 in the Maracanã.

The Libertadores victory changed the outlook for Brazilian teams. Episodically, clubs like Santos and Cruzeiro had their runs and went away. Now clubs could aspire to win both the Libertadores and the world title. The year 1981 put Flamengo on the map; they beat Europe's crown jewel of a side. Without this win, Grêmio a couple of years later wouldn't have the experience to ready themselves for a similar assault.

Chapter 3

Fla–Flu Rivalry

A BOOK about Flamengo wouldn't be complete without talking about the Fla–Flu rivalry.[24] Like any other derby or rivalry, this has had its strange points – matches or outside stimuli that have put some weight on the match. Most of the time it has been a war or politicians trying to exercise their will on society. From the end of 2019 until the end of 2020 the world was shut down to stop the spread of COVID-19. There were many times where matches had to be played behind closed doors, and during this era every club had to play with either reduced fans or none.

Also, during 2019 Flamengo were in another of their golden eras, as they won the national title, reached the quarter-final of the Copa do Brasil, won the Copa Libertadores and reached the final of the Club World Cup against Liverpool. It was a remake of the 1981 season with some minor changes, one being that Liverpool actually took the match seriously this time and won, the other being the Zico of this iteration of Flamengo wasn't one of the world's best players – Gabigol is just good enough. Over the 2020

---

24 https://worldfootballindex.com/2020/07/fluminense-flamengo-preview-a-flu-fla-battle-like-no-other/

edition of the derby, Flamengo won 3-2 against Fluminense in matches.

The great Tim Vickery,[25] a pundit that many in the football supporting culture know very well, waxed prophetic in *World Soccer* magazine about the Fla–Flu derby:

> The Fla–Flu is probably Rio's most glamorous derby. But it cannot claim to be the biggest. Because if Flamengo are the most popular club, then Vasco da Gama are in second place. Indeed, the Fla–Vasco clash is known as 'the derby of the multitudes'. Even so, the Fla–Flu has a grip on the imagination. The country's current political polarization, for example, is often referred to as a Fla–Flu divide. Part of this may be down to the pleasing phonetics. But the appeal of the Fla–Flu has much to do with the way that football was popularized in Brazil, the form that myths were invented and traditions created.

That's the key to the sport – every big city in the football-developed world has an intercity derby. Most are famous too, anywhere from Glasgow with Celtic versus Rangers, North London with Tottenham versus Arsenal, Milan with Inter versus AC Milan, and Buenos Aires with Boca Juniors versus River Plate. The same can be said for the second-biggest city in Brazil, Rio, and it's one of the oldest in the game. The abbreviation Fla–Flu was created by Mário Fihlo to reflect the conflict between the two clubs. There are

---

25 www.worldsoccer.com/columnists/tim-vickery-columnists/tim-vickerys-notes-from-south-america-brief-history-of-the-flamengo-fluminense-derby-369381

other big clubs in Rio, like Botafogo and Vasco da Gama, but it's impossible to tell the story of any of these without including the others.

We have talked at length about the beginning of Flamengo, and that they were created by a breakaway group from Fluminense. Arthur Cox started Fluminense and, like Flamengo's founders, he did play. In the first game they beat Rio FC 8-0, while Cox scored a hat-trick. He was also part of the side that won their first title, the 1906 Campeonato Carioca. From the early days of Fluminense, they were a team of the upper class of Rio thanks to their English roots. Normally, you would see supporters dressed in top-of-the-line clothing. As was a sign of the times, black or mixed-race players were prohibited from playing for them. They did have a mixed-race player but he covered his face with rice powder so he could play.

It was extreme, but soon it was a policy with the club, like the Protestant-only rule Glasgow Rangers had. Fluminense supporters embraced the idea and created songs celebrating the fact; even today, rice powder is thrown around seeking to create an atmosphere. Flamengo were the opposite and became a club for all the people, mostly from the working and lower classes. This approach connected with the fans better, making them the best-supported club in the country. Fla–Flu is such a unique derby and encounter in Brazil. There isn't a division between religion or politics; it's just a matter of pride.

There have been some great clashes between the two clubs over the decades; one of the most remembered is an encounter in 1963 when 194,000 filled the Maracanã Stadium. At the time, it was the third-biggest attendance after the *Maracanazo*, the 1950 World Cup Final between

Brazil and Uruguay, and a match between Brazil and Paraguay four years later. Unfortunately, the match between Flamengo and Fluminense ended 0-0.

Just as tiresome as the Barcelona versus Real Madrid derby, Flamengo and Fluminense can meet at least three times a year due to all the competitions they enter. In 1916, Fla–Flu became one of the first matches ever to be suspended in Carioca league history because of a pitch invasion by Fluminense fans after a referee allowed Flamengo to retake a penalty three times. Many decades later in 1941, the derby was a battle for the title. Flamengo needed a win to take the title, while a draw was all that Fluminense needed. Towards the end of the first half, Fluminense led 2-1 before conceding a late equaliser.

Then, like in most important matches, events took a dramatic turn. The Flamengo stadium – this was a decade before the Maracanã – was in the middle of Rodrigo de Freitas Lagoon, which meant that when a ball flew out of the stadium it would land in open water. Fluminense's players took advantage of this and overhit shots out of the ground on purpose to waste time. Flamengo anticipated this beforehand, and their board ordered rowers to be stationed in the lagoon to return the ball quicker. The move failed to pay off as Fluminense held on and won the title. They have met many times since then, but the most famous came well after Flamengo conquered the world.

In the 1995 game, the derby was called 'the belly game'. This was again in the Campeonato Carioca during a rainy day at the Maracanã. Fluminense went in at half-time with a 2-0 lead, with goals from Renato Gaúcho and Leonardo. Flamengo came back in the second half and levelled, with goals from Romário and Fabinho. With the flow of the game going Flamengo's way, it looked like nothing could stop them, until three minutes from time when Renato Gaúcho's attempt came in. Renato, in a clearly offside position, deflected a cross into the net with his belly to win Fluminense the title. The goal, however, was credited to Aílton, who had crossed the ball into the box.

For Fluminense, Renato Gaúcho is one of the most important names in the club's history, along with Telê Santana and Rivellino. Just like with other great rivalries, many stars have represented both sides of the divide, including such greats as Romário and Ronaldinho. Nowadays, in 2021, Ganso and Gabriel Barbosa have taken up the mantle for the clubs. While the derby has retained the same passion, the clubs have had different fortunes in the 2000s.

Fluminense have struggled: they have failed to win a trophy since 2012 and have been at the bottom of the league. Flamengo, on the other hand, won the Copa Libertadores in 2019, and played Liverpool in the Club World Cup. They were led by ex-Benfica coach Jorge Jesus, and had goalkeeper Diego Alves and full-backs Rafinha and Filipe Luís. This victory added to the league they had won comfortably. But no matter how different their form is, the passion and intensity of this rivalry will always endure.[26]

Ever since the first derby, the rivalry has been part of the footballing culture and identity of Rio. The match has become synonomous with a packed Maracanã, and with the excitement of fans from around the world and Brazil. The spiritual home of Brazil is the Maracanã, and when it's at its most effervescent is during the build-up to Fla–Flu.

---

26 https://beyondthelastman.com/2020/11/13/fla-v-flu-the-divide-in-rio-de-janeiro/

The Maracanã is a symbol of the rivalry, but the footballing amphitheatre, which opened in 1950, didn't start hosting the match until 1963. That match was far from a memorable one as it was 0-0, handing the Rio State title to Flamengo. The only remarkable thing about the match was that almost 200,000 attended. One person in the stands? A young Zico and his family.

Before the Maracanã, some of the matches took on mythical auras, an example being the famous *'Fla–Flu da Lagoa'* or 'Fla–Flu of the Lake' for the Rio Championships on 23 November 1941. This was held in Flamengo's stadium next to the Lagoa Rodrigo de Freitas, a large lake in southern Rio. The Rio State Championship was on the line, as Zizinho opened the scoring for Flamengo. Then it turned into Fluminense's match as they tied it up, and then put themselves ahead 2-1. Fluminense were cruising towards the title, until the 84th minute when Flamengo equalised.

Flamengo set their eyes on a final devastating assault on Fluminense's goal. Fluminense goalkeeper Batatais had broken his collarbone, but couldn't be substituted as they weren't allowed during this era. So to stop the onslaught, rumour has it, the Fluminense players decided to kick the ball into the river. Each time the referee asked for a reserve ball, Flamengo employees would jump into the lake for the ball and the Fluminense players would say the ball was too wet to play. The referee became very mad at this and sent off Fluminense striker Carreiro for time-wasting. Carreiro took his time leaving the field. The minutes ticked by and the match ended in a 2-2 tie – Fluminense had won the league in a strange way.

One of the great tools in writing is social networking because it can be sourced for research on niche topics.

Flamengo is one of if not the best-supported club in Brazil, but they are still a niche subject outside South America. One of the questions I've asked Flamengo supporters is what is the most memorable Fla–Flu match, to which I have got a lot of answers. The 1963 Carioca Final on 15 December 1963 in the Maracanã was seen by 194,603 people,[27] a record for the derby in the Maracanã. Also, the club won the title from this match.

---

27 https://livroanacao.blogspot.com/search?q=1963

Chapter 4

Troubled Times in Brazil

SOUTH AMERICA has always had its troubled areas and regimes, and Brazil has had its fair share of hard times. The military held power from 1964 until March 1985, when it completely fell apart due to struggles in the regime. Changes in regime of 1889, 1930 and 1945 unleashed competing political forces and splits in the military, like the change of 1964. No civilian politician was acceptable to the various factions so the army chief of staff, Marshal Humberto Castelo Branco, became president. His goal was to reform the political-economic system. He refused to stay beyond the term of João Goulart, who the military had deposed.

His policies didn't work out, as military coups don't tend to, as hardliners wanted a complete purge of left-wing and populist influencers, and civilian politicians obstructed Castelo Branco's reforms, accusing him of dictatorial methods. When he decided to appease the hardliners, he recessed, then purged Congress. He removed objectionable state governors, and decreed the expansion of the president's arbitrary powers at the expense of the other branches of government. He did curb the populist left, but the successor governments of Marshal Artur da Costa e Silva (1967–69) and General Emílio Garrastazu Médici (1969–74) formed the basis for authoritarian rule. The opposition party understood this too late to force any change. Despite all of this, Castelo Branco tried to maintain a degree of democracy, and his economic reforms paved the way for the Brazilian economic miracle of the next decade. Also, his restructuring of the party system shaped the government opposition relations for the next two decades.

The factions became armed officers who would confine themselves to their army duties and hardliners who wanted to continue fighting against the politicians. The concern for appearances meant that they had to keep a face that they weren't a dictatorship, so they required each president to pass the power to his replacement.

Anytime there's a regime change or a revolution in the world, one has to wonder who the superpowers are behind it. The United States is behind a lot of global regime changes, directly or indirectly, depending on which scholar you listen to. An anti-Goulart press campaign in 1963 and 1964 received moral support from the Lyndon Johnson administration. It was later found out that Ambassador Lincoln Gordon had given money to the anti-Goulart candidates in the 1962 elections. Furthermore, the Americans encouraged the plotters, and used extra American military, intelligence personnel and four Navy oil tankers in an operation code-named 'Brother Sam'.

The government in Washington DC immediately recognised the new Brazilian government in 1964 and joined the chorus, saying that it had staved off the communism infecting the world. The Americans were the only foreign hands involved, albeit indirectly. On 13 December 1968, the Brazilian president enacted the Fifth Institutional Act, gave himself dictatorial powers, dissolved Congress and state legislatures, suspended the constitution and imposed censorship.

In October 1969, President Costa e Silva died, and the officer corps chose General Garrastazu Médici as president. The hardline faction of the military wanted to hold authority as long as necessary. The Médici government showed how it was possible to hold power without support, a party or a programme. There were many terrorist actions in the cities, kidnappings of diplomats including the United States ambassador and an extensive anti-guerrilla campaign in Goiás.

The repressive agenda spilled into various other agencies, and they spied, used dirty tricks and torture, and disappeared on their political opponents. This all finally caused a break between the government and the Roman Catholic Church. The annual GDP growth rate was at 12 per cent, so that was possible, though there was great civil disobedience in the streets as this was all ramping up, as we will get to later in the chapter.

It was against this backdrop that retired General Ernesto Geisel came to power in 1974. At the time, it wasn't known how Geisel's accession would help, but it was a move away from repression towards democracy. He replaced many regional commanders and instituted a programme of gradual relaxation of authoritarian rule. President Geisel sought to maintain high economic growth, and investments in infrastructure, highways, telecommunications, hydroelectric dams, factories and atomic energy.

Then in 1977 and 1978, succession issues came up again, so Geisel attempted in April 1977 to restrain the growing opposition by creating an electoral college to approve his selected replacement. He allowed the return of exiles, restored habeas corpus and repealed the extraordinary powers decreed by the Fifth Institutional Act. And he appointed General João Figueiredo as his successor in March 1979.

The last military president, João Figueiredo, took the presidency out of a sense of duty rather than political ambition. He signed a general amnesty into law and opened up the political system to make the country a democracy. Soaring inflation, declining productivity and a mounting foreign debt, however, plagued his presidency. To attack the soaring debt, he put an emphasis on exports: food, natural resources, automobiles, arms, clothing, shoes and even electricity. Americans were kept at arm's length from all of this.

A book on Brazilian soccer would not be complete without some events of the time. The 1980s were a time of overindulgence, more of a 'give me, it's mine' generation, which has shown its consequences many decades later. However, in South America it was a time of oppression and dictatorships. Argentina was going through a military dictatorship. The military in Brazil held power from 1964 to March of 1985.

The history of the republic, as we have seen earlier, shows the development of the military as a national institution. With the elimination of the monarchy, national institutions were reduced to one, the army. The Roman Catholic Church was present throughout the country; it was not national but rather international with its personnel, doctrines, liturgy and purposes. Because of the military dictatorship, there weren't political parties.

The army became the core of the developing Brazilian state by the early 1980s, which occurred haphazardly after the collapse of the monarchy. Most of the army was stationed in Rio de Janeiro and Rio Grande do Sul, but its presence, personal interests, ideology and commitments were felt nationwide.

The hardliners didn't like the idea of the democracy and set off a series of terrorist bombings. That's where the May Day bombing in 1981 came from. Figueiredo proved to be too weak to punish the guilty, and promised the public he would end the military rule. That just added to the other problems weighing on his government, like soaring inflation, declining productivity and mounting foreign debt.

Political liberalisation and a regressing world economy contributed to Brazil's economic and social problems. In 1978 and 1980 there were huge strikes in the industrial rings around São Paulo. Protesters asserted that wage increases didn't meet the cost of living; in fact they were far below the threshold of living. Union leaders, which included 1990 presidential candidate Luiz Inácio da Silva, were arrested on violation of national security laws. As a result of this, the International Monetary Fund (IMF) imposed a strict austerity programme on Brazil. Brazil was required to hold down wages to fight the inflation and people seized unused private land, which meant the government had to form a new land-reform ministry.

To bring down the debt, Figueiredo's administration exported everything it could. This was also helped by the establishment of ties with any country that wanted to contribute to Brazil's economic development. In a rare instance, Washington DC was kept at a distance from this process. In order to explain the events of the May Day parade attack, we need to set the stage.

The events took place on 31 April 1981 during the May Day parade in Rio at the Convention Center, and the result was that the Federal Public Prosecution indicted five military men and a police chief with the lawsuit that was the Riocentro case. Retired Generals Newton Cruz, Nilton Cerqueira, and retired Colonel Wilson Luiz Chaves Machado, and former police chief Claudio Antonio Guerra were charged with first-degree murder with aggravated circumstances, criminal conspiracy with the use of weapons and carrying explosives. Newton Cruz was also indicted on cronyism. Retired General Edson Sá Rocha was indicted on criminal conspiracy with the use of a weapon. Retired Major Divany Carvalho Barros was charged with procedural fraud.

The Riocentro bombing killed Sergeant Guilherme Pereira do Rosário, who was sitting next to Wilson Machado inside a car. Surprisingly, Machado survived despite the car being destroyed. Yet another bomb went off inside the Riocentro powerhouse during a concert – 20,000 people were in attendance. The Riocentro case was opened twice by the Military Court, in 1981 and 1991, with no results. It was reopened because more information was found, most of it testimonials of people who saw the military handling the bomb inside the car and the bomb in the concert hall. Many experts have argued that justice needs to be done in military dictatorships and their crimes to restore truth and trust in society.

The inclusion of this history is to show the political and societal problems facing Rio at the time, making the run by Flamengo not only good for the club but also for the community. Life in the 70s and 80s wasn't as glamorous as some have implied. In times of strife, a glamorous club could bring a community together.

Chapter 5

Brazil, Sport and Culture

CULTURALLY, FOOTBALL is in everyone's soul from day one. Many people are given a football as their first gift. Kids grow up wanting to be the next Pelé, Zico, Nunes, Júnior, Romário, Garrincha or Ronaldo. To say that football is important is an understatement; in some aspects, it's just as important as religion.

Football in Brazil is a dance, mostly known as the samba style in football. All of this has its roots in Africa, where, as we mentioned earlier, the crown imported slaves from. It's linked to the African dance of capoeira, developed in Brazil as a form of cultural resistance. American slaves did the same with the songs in the fields, and you can see why all over the world the ruling class looked down on football. Low-class sport was just a racial division aspect of the time.

Football is a sport of the middle and lower classes; that isn't in dispute. It's a sport that doesn't need too much practice, just some type of ball, some form of field and goals. As we have seen, players have had to be creative to practise their sport. We've heard of some players making footballs out of socks, some using oranges and others using chairs as goals. The only thing really holding a vast majority of people back from going far in the sport is money. It brings all races and classes together from all corners of the world.

One could hazard a guess that there are more football pitches than churches in Rio, and they would probably be right. With Brazil being a poor country, not many of these pitches are top of the line; some, if not many, are falling apart. It's the holes in the pitch that help the players learn to play the beautiful game. The passing and dribbling styles that have come to dominate the Brazilian game are from playing on pitches like this.

The Brazilian national team are considered the top of the sport, and with their five World Cups, it's right to think that. It took a long time for them to get on that pedestal, even with some bumps in the road. The obvious bump in the road for Brazil was hosting the 1950 World Cup and losing in the final to Uruguay 2-1, which was immortalised as the '*Maracanazo*'. Brazil got to usher in a great era eight years later when Santos legend Pelé at 17, along with Garrincha brought home their first World Cup, in Sweden. From then on, Brazil kept up the pace as being one of the greatest countries in the world.

They won the World Cup in 1958, 1962, 1970, 1994 and 2002. In fact, they are so good that the 1982 team is still talked of, as Stuart Horsfield said: 'The 1982 Brazilian World Cup side were a team that never even made it to a semi-final, and yet their impact was instant and timeless'.[28] A book about the side not winning the World Cup was produced many decades later. That was an investment in a niche topic because so many people are still interested in the nostalgia of the sport.

---

28 *1982 Brazil: The Glorious Failure* – Stuart Horsfield

In the Brazilian Confederation (CBF), there are 501 pro clubs among the four national divisions, and 13,000 amateur clubs in the country. That's a massive number of clubs dedicated to football. Brazil also has leagues in 26 states and the Federal District, and most of the amateur teams are in the lowlands.

When the World Cup is held, every four years, many countries go on holiday to watch it. While there are many problems in Brazil, all hope is put on the men's team winning the World Cup.[29] With all this on their backs, you can see why the sport is so stressful for players, and to a point why they have to play overseas. Football isn't well funded in the country.

When the Portuguese colonised Brazil, they wanted to tear away the Brazilians from all their cultural practices in order to westernise them. They had no idea they were initiating the growth of the beautiful game. As we know, football came from the United Kingdom and spread from there. Each society took to the sport in a unique way, and contributed to its growth.

The Brazilian contribution to the sport was dribbling, speed and creativity. Ginga, as it's called, is like a rhythmic dance, and generations were born into it. Brazilians moved with a style that showed the art and culture of the day. Football became more than a game to them; it was a symbol of freedom and hope for every kid on the streets of Rio. To this point, futsal had played a big part in its growth and embraced the creativity the Brazilians needed for their football. Pelé even used futsal, saying it made people think, play fast. The national team not only captures the hearts of

---

29 http://eltecolote.org/content/en/sports-2/brazil-and-soccer-a-love-story/

the Brazilian citizens but also people worldwide. It took over the world, mostly because they only played their matches out of the country.

In a country that sees a lot of pain and suffering, the national team shows what unity and togetherness does for a group of people. There is a certain aspect of religion to the sport in Brazil – over the years we have seen Brazilian players fall to the ground and praise God for a win. Some have even gone further for injuries and other problems. The idea of football being more than just scoring and defending was also ingrained in their heads. This is what became a religion, what their passion and belief was based on.

Chapter 6

Intercontinental Cup

BEFORE THERE was the Club World Cup, there was the Intercontinental Cup. For a good majority of it, the European clubs didn't think too much of it; often, the European Cup winner would skip it altogether. In fact, during the 1970s Liverpool had done such a thing, and Brian Clough skipped the first one his Nottingham Forest side were scheduled to play in. Ironically, they played the following one in 1980, losing to Nacional of Uruguay. And they were all skipping the tournament because of the 1966 World Cup.

The story of this, however, starts a decade before, in 1958. During the Congress of the South American Football Confederation (CONMEBOL), in Rio de Janeiro of all places, the president of UEFA, Henri Delaunay, proposed a competition between the top clubs in Europe. Out of this came the Copa Libertadores for South America, as the mechanism for South American clubs. The European Cup had been around for three years before this Congress. Its winner would face the winner of the European Cup, starting in 1960, and it would be called the Intercontinental Cup.

The first seven editions of the Intercontinental Cup saw many great European sides, from Real Madrid, Benfica and AC Milan. In the South American part of the tournament, great clubs like Santos and Peñarol were showing Europe that there were very good players to be had. The standard of play was generally pretty high.

A big year for the competition was 1966. It was the first time that domestic runners-up were allowed into the Copa Libertadores, which angered Brazilian clubs. That meant great clubs like Pelé's Santos were kept out, for the most part leaving Argentine and Uruguayan teams to win. This would parachute them into the Intercontinental Cup.

The 1966 World Cup also plays into this, as the Brazilians were kicked against all three of the European teams they played. They didn't make it out of the group stage. Argentina were angry too, as England's manager Alf Ramsey called the players animals after captain Antonio Rattín was sent off. So meetings between the two continents were temperamental at best, which set off the next meetings in the Intercontinental Cup.

Also, there was the Intercontinental Cup match the year before between Racing Club and Scottish outfit Celtic. The three-legged tie turned into a slugfest, a dirty match at both ends of the field. The final game, which saw Racing Club triumph, has infamously been dubbed 'The Battle of Montevideo' after a terribly violent game. Three players from the Scottish side and two from the Argentine side were sent off in a game that was interrupted by riot police on numerous occasions. A fourth Celtic player was also dismissed, but amid the chaos he stayed on the pitch and escaped having to leave the field.

In 1968, after winning the European Cup and Copa Libertadores respectively, Manchester United and Estudiantes de La Plata were pitted against each other. Manchester United manager Sir Matt Busby was expecting a hostile reaction and, indeed, that is exactly what his team got when the first leg of the final was played in Argentina on 25 September 1968, after a warm welcome in Argentina from the receiving dignitaries.

Prior to the match, a bomb that released red smoke was set off in the stadium, which proved what many people knew: the crowds in South America were exciting, and different from anything Manchester United had seen on their travels.

The South American club played dirty and ultimately won on the night 1-0 thanks to a strike from Marcos Conigliaro. Nobby Stiles in particular had a night to forget after being sent off in the 79th minute. Stiles retaliated after being targeted by the opposition with kicks, punches and even headbutts throughout the match, presumably as retribution for the World Cup exit two years prior. His red card meant that he would be suspended for the return leg in Manchester. Bobby Charlton also had to leave the field after receiving a severe head injury that needed stitches.

The final and deciding match was in the British Isles, at Old Trafford on 16 October. There were 300 Argentinians who had made it to the match, with 63,000 United supporters also filling the famous stadium. Tickets for the highly anticipated game were anywhere from £3 to ten shillings, and gate receipts totalling £50,000 were a record for that time. Just like the first match, the second, in driving Manchester rain, was a niggly affair. After Juan Ramón Verón put the ball in the back of the United net in the sixth minute, the home side needed to score three goals to win the tie and two to force a play-off.

The game boiled over once more at the end, with George Best punching defender José Medina and pushing Néstor Togneri to the ground. Yugoslavian referee Konstantin

Zečević sent off both Medina and Best, with both having to be escorted to the opposing dressing rooms. Outside-right Willie Morgan did manage to get a consolation goal in the 90th minute but it wasn't enough. Estudiantes had come to Europe and won the cup, in England, and at Old Trafford. The Estudiantes players tried to do a lap of honour after winning the match, but the supporters who had stayed hurled anything they could find at the players as they were parading around.

A couple of years later, Manchester United suffered the same treatment against Estudiantes. In 1969, for the third year running, an Argentinian club would be South America's representatives, this time against European giants AC Milan. Estudiantes had won the year before against Manchester United, thanks to a 1-1 draw in the second leg at Old Trafford after winning 1-0 at the iconic La Bombonera in Buenos Aires.

What happened in Buenos Aires in 1969 changed the Intercontinental Cup for the rest of its existence. The Argentinians tried to live up to their reputation of the 1966 World Cup, where they were labelled as the most physical nation in world football. The cup was a two-legged series, with the first match being held on 8 October 1969 in the San Siro. This match was a complete disaster for the Argentinian side, as Milan, who had won the European Cup earlier in the year, put three goals into the back of the net.

One of the goals came via Argentina-born, French international Néstor Combin, who scored a goal in the 45th minute of the game to put the Italians 2-0 up against his countrymen. An Angelo Sormani brace meant that the first leg ended 3-0 to the Milan club, which would be an almost insurmountable scoreline in the return leg in South America.

It was the return match that really put this tie into the history books. On 22 October, the two clubs met in Boca Juniors' home stadium, La Bombonera, for the deciding match. Estudiantes were already down by three goals, and it would be a massive task for them to turn around the tie. All of that must have played in the minds of the players when they went out on to the field. The police did nothing to quell the fans or the opposing club from bending the rules, or harassing the players. While Milan were in the tunnel, hot coffee was being poured all over them. Fans threw things on to the field at the Italian giants, and while Milan were warming up, Estudiantes kicked balls at them.

What has always been obvious is that South American referees are known to turn a blind eye to a lot of things. The Chilean referee, Massaro, had a shocking match. None of the Milan players received any preferential treatment; they all had their fair share of fouls and hard play. In the early moments of the match, Pierino Prati was taken down very harshly by an Estudiantes player, which gave Prati concussion.

Milan captain Gianni Rivera was abused by goalkeeper Alberto Poletti, in retaliation for scoring the opener in the 4-0 aggregate scoreline. Néstor Combin took so much heavy treatment that he was left bloodied and needed medical treatment after a Ramón Suárez elbow. While he was getting medical attention, the Argentine police arrested him for dodging military service when he moved to Europe to play football. While Estudiantes won the match 2-1 with goals from Marcos Conigliaro and Suárez in the dying moments of the first half, they lost the tie 4-2 on aggregate.

The media lost its mind and rightfully so after the match. Both the Italian and the Argentine press called the Estudiantes players a national embarrassment, referring to the match as a 90-minute witch hunt and wanting action taken against Estudiantes. Even the Argentine government got involved: military dictator Juan Onganía demanded that punishments be handed out. As a result, the Argentinian FA gave Ramón Suárez and Eduardo Manero bans upwards of 30 matches, and the goalkeeper Poletti was banned for life.

This match ruined the competition, and over the next ten years most European clubs boycotted it. Estudiantes would go on to the next edition to face Dutch team Feyenoord, losing again, this time in a much closer 3-2 aggregate defeat. It would be the final time Estudiantes would take part in the cup. Ajax would win the European Cup in 1971, but declined entry to the Continental Cup, which meant that Greek club Panathinaikos were to play Nacional of Uruguay. And what became of Néstor Combin? He was released from jail after two days and returned to Italy, before playing out his career in France with Metz and then Red Star Belgrade.

The need to claim to be the best team in the world has tormented football since the World Cup and the Olympics began. So there had to be a competition to decide it. The Intercontinental Cup, while not being perfect, was the one. In the 60s, one of the great sides in the sport was Argentina's Independiente. They were like Liverpool – between them they had won 11 European Cups and Copa Libertadores between 1964 and 1984. Independiente won the Intercontinental Cup in 1973 and the fans loved every moment of it. For all Liverpool's achievements in the 60s, 70s and 80s,[30] the Intercontinental Cup was the only trophy the club had never won.

---

30 www.fourfourtwo.com/features/liverpool-flamengo-club-world-cup-1981-1984-independiente-intercontinental-cup

But most European sides had declined to play in it due to how rough the Argentine sides were. The English legacy in the cup, however, was netted by a Scot, Willie Morgan, for Manchester United. That, however, did not help the fact they had not won a match in the competition. The clubs who had been partaking in the cup were a who's who of great sides at the time: Matt Busby's Manchester United, Tony Barton's Aston Villa and Brian Clough's Nottingham Forest. But they had all fallen to clubs like Estudiantes, Nacional and Peñarol.

Often, wins for the South American sides weren't because the teams were better than the European teams. European teams were often kicked off the pitch for retailiation against the physical play of the South American teams. While losing at Estudiantes in 1968, George Best claimed firecrackers were flung at him. Never to be shown up, he subsequently returned the favour by punching an opponent in the second leg at Old Trafford. It wasn't the only incident, as Alex Stepney later presented the referee with a thrown bottle that had almost found its target.

Independiente themselves were no angels. During a match against Herrera's Grande Inter in Buenos Aires, the crowd hit the Milan players with rocks. Liverpool, hearing about all of this, refused to participate in 1977 and 1978, as did Nottingham Forest in 1979.

In setting the scene for the Flamengo versus Liverpool match, we do have to talk about Liverpool. At the time of the match, the club were in their glory period. This had stretched from the 1970s into the 1980s, and during that time four managers took the side into finals. Bill Shankly started the ascent in 1959, Bob Paisley took it up a notch, Joe

Fagan steadied the ship and player-manager Kenny Dalglish kept it going until the end.

By the time Flamengo and Liverpool met in Tokyo, Bill Shankly had died. His trusty assistant Bob Paisley, who didn't want the job to begin with, took over. In the middle of the 1970s, he became one of the greats. While big names like Don Revie, Brian Clough and Jock Stein were mentioned as greats, Paisley was happy going about his business. Bob was a quiet man and by the time he assumed the manager's job, he had filled many roles at the club. He was, as he said, just filling in until a proper manager came around. The job filler ended up winning 19 trophies in almost nine seasons: six league titles, three European Cups, a UEFA Cup, three League Cups, five Charity Shields and one European Super Cup. Bob is the only manager with three European Cups with the same club, and that's even considering he only managed until the mid-80s.

Long before Kenny Dalglish became a medal-winning manager, he was a medal-winning player. In 1977, he came from Celtic, after a stellar career in Scotland, to replace Kevin Keegan who had gone to Hamburg. Paisley coached him to be one of the greatest players for the Reds, but it wasn't a one-man show. Ian Rush was picked up from Chester City, Bruce Grobbelaar came in from Vancouver in the North American Soccer League and Mark Lawrenson, Alan Kennedy and Graeme Souness were all brought in.

No matter the players, the medals kept coming in. Paisley won the league in 1976, 1977, 1979, 1980, 1982 and 1983, the League Cup from 1981 to 1983, the European Cup in 1977, 1978 and 1981, the UEFA Cup in 1976 and the UEFA Super Cup in 1977. That haul alone made him one of the greatest managers of all time in the UK. Most will talk about Alex Ferguson, and he was one of the great managers as well. The reason for all the success was the collectiveness of the play on the pitch. They defended and attacked together, which was known as 'the Liverpool way', and it was taught at all levels of the club from the first team to the reserve team, making it easy to churn out talent. They could switch from possession to counter-attacking. It was devastating.

Unlike many tactical advancements, the brand of football was purposeful. Attacking was the key; possession wasn't to be wasted. Case in point: the 1977 European Super Cup. In a counter-attack move right out of a training-ground exercise, Phil Neal cut off a pass meant for Hamburg's Ferdinand Keller, then found an open Ray Kennedy, who exploited the open space to dribble into. He then played it in for Terry McDermott who scored the third goal of the match. The entire sequence took three passes.

Another part of 'the Liverpool way' was splicing fitness and tactics in practice, which was Paisley's strong point. He was the man who developed five-a-sides in training to help hone in on the touch-and-go football that they needed to play during matches. The whole training system was reworked with Paisley, and he mandated methodical cool-down practices after training and matchdays. Much of Liverpool's success was based on the hard work each player put in for the common good. Each player was told and expected to never be bigger than the club or their team-mates. Players were transferred out before they were a detriment to the team. You had to be able to help the club.

The quiet man that Paisley was, he knew he didn't have to tangle with the press, or boast that he was right. The results were the proof of why he was right, and this was from a manager who averaged two pieces of silverware a year. If you look back on the wins, it's not that they won, it's how Liverpool won. That's because he wanted you to win, and then figure out how you played. Being arrogant wasn't a trait common to the club or the city of Liverpool. This type of culture lasted at Liverpool long after Paisley, because he made winning a habit.

Part of the reason Liverpool were so good during the late 70s and 80s was the tandem of Kenny Dalglish and Ian Rush. They became so good that people wondered, like they did with Kevin Keegan and John Toshack, if they were operating on telepathy. This was funny considering Rush professed later on that, in the early days, he hated Dalglish, because Kenny was famous for his trash-talking and locker-room camaraderie. This was generally how Dalglish would help get the new players to assimilate into the collective as quickly as possible. Either you sank or you swam, and Rush almost sank. Eventually, though, Rush was the one trash-talking. The goals flew in, the medals were collected and many miles were traversed collecting all the accolades.

For as many goals as flew in, you had to defend. Alan Hansen and Mark Lawrenson made the side all-conquering. Hansen and Lawrenson were together for six and a half seasons before the recurrence of Lawrenson's Achilles injury against Arsenal forced him to retire at 30. Lawrenson was so talented that he could be played all over the field. He was the perfect foil for Hansen, as he was so comfortable with the ball, and had great speed, which is why the Achilles injury put him out. Hansen had a sense for positioning and was in some respects even more comfortable with the ball than Lawrenson was.

In 1977 Paisley brought Hanson from Partick Thistle and made serious inroads into signing Lawrenson, who was at Preston North End in the Third Division. Paisley wasn't ready to pay the £100,000 asking price for someone who hadn't made 100 professional appearances nor in the top two divisions yet. Lawrenson instead moved to Brighton and Hove Albion for the time being, and helped them reach the top flight for the first time in their history two years later. Lawrenson made his way to Anfield in 1981, and Liverpool ended up paying nine times over the £100,000 asking price.

Alan Hansen started out his career trying to break the Emlyn Hughes and Phil Thompson partnership. This forced him to start his career at Anfield as the fourth-choice centre-back. Hansen had to contend with the legend of Tommy Smith, and Joey Jones. By the end of his first season at the club, he was moving up the chart due to the uneven play of Jones, and Smith dropping an axe on his foot, ending his own chance of playing in the European Cup Final of 1981. Ironically, the Hansen and Thompson partnership was just as beautiful as Hansen and Lawrenson. Lawrenson himself made his debut in August 1981 at left-back in place of Alan Kennedy. Lawrenson's career-ending injury was one of the first cracks in the foundation of the Liverpool dynasty. Not being able to replace him brought the whole thing down eventually.

Of course, to link the back players you have to have a great midfield, and throughout the years Liverpool had many great players roaming the midfield. For Liverpool fans of a certain generation, Graeme Souness was the best midfielder they ever saw. And to think he was the property of two clubs, Tottenham and Middlesbrough, who could have used him. For most people, Souness was a hardman, and more on that later, but in the European Cup in 1978 against Club Brugge, Souness side-footed a diagonal pass through the right side of the Club Brugge penalty area to Kenny Dalglish, who put the ball into the back of the net to retain the European Cup. This was all done by Souness with limited space to spare and while being stared at by René Vandereycken. Souness's style of playing could be considered a punch, but it was more like time standing still and then being thrown forward.

Souness won countless cups and titles in his time at Anfield, but the true mark of his impact on the team was how he could see the club through tough times. He was made captain during the 1981/82 season, which was very unLiverpool like, as they were sitting in 12th place in the league on Boxing Day 1981. Yet by the following May, they were champions. In the 1984 League Cup Final replay, Souness scored the winning goal against Everton.

Liverpool have had a string of great goalkeepers dating all the way back to Elisha Scott before World War One. From Tommy Lawrence to Ray Clemence to Bruce Grobbelaar, these players are the stuff of legends. Bruce Grobbelaar was a great player – very few can argue that. His list of honours was also impressive with six league titles, three FA Cups, three League Cups and a European Cup.

The common stereotype of goalkeepers being a little bit crazy can be applied to Grobbelaar. He was more than just a goalkeeper; in fact, he was an all-round sportsman. Growing up in South Africa, he excelled at both cricket and basketball, but it wasn't until he picked up a football that he began to make his name. However, while he was doing that, he was conscripted into the Rhodesian army through national service. This was the time of the Rhodesian Bush

War, and the fight for independence. Grobbelaar was fighting for the white-minority government of Ian Smith against Robert Mugabe's African National Union. The atrocities that Grobbelaar took part in haunt him to this day.

Once he was discharged, he was able to resume his career in football. This was a long, strange journey. First, he played in Canada for the North American Soccer League's Vancouver Whitecaps. His play there earned him a trial at West Bromwich Albion, but he failed to get a contract. Bruce finally latched on with a club known for development in Crewe Alexandra. He lasted only two thirds of a season before being spotted by Liverpool scout Tom Saunders. Saunders recommended him to Bob Paisley and, in March 1981, Grobbelaar was signed as cover for Ray Clemence.

Part of the Liverpool way was that each new signing got an apprenticeship of at least two years in the reserves. That was expected for Grobbelaar, but football tends to take people by surprise. Suddenly, in the summer of 1981, Ray Clemence announced that he wanted to leave the club. Grobbelaar was now thrust into the spotlight like no other. What a season to get thrown into, 1981/82 for Liverpool. The defence also had some trouble getting used to the new style that Grobbelaar brought to the game. Clemence would organise the defence and stay in his goal, whereas Grobbelaar would not hesitate coming out for a corner kick.

Grobbelaar's style of play came into focus in the mid-point of the season, as on Boxing Day 1981 Liverpool were beaten 3-1 at home by Manchester City. He was responsible for at least two of the goals. This put his place in jeopardy, but the scouts couldn't find a capable player so Grobbelaar played on. And he did improve, leading Liverpool to a First Division title and League Cup double.

While Grobbelaar was steady between the pipes, he wasn't immune to high-profile mistakes. In consecutive seasons, his errors eliminated Liverpool from the European Cup. At one point, Bob Bolder was brought in from Sheffield Wednesday to challenge Bruce. However, the Zimbabwean was such a reliable hand on the line-up sheet that he didn't miss a match for five years. He was injured in the 1986 FA Charity Shield against Everton, and was forced to miss the first few matches of the season. He was also injured at the end of the season, forcing Liverpool to concede the title to Everton.

While this was a team of stars, one who shone brightly throughout the late 70s and 80s was Kenny Dalglish. He was very good and very fast as a youth, and was part of the 'Quality Street Gang' group of young players Celtic brought through as the Lisbon Lions were getting older. As a youth, he had trials with two or three clubs, ironically including one for Liverpool, but they sent him back. Stein sent him on loan to Cumbernauld United for first-team football. Kenny hit 37 goals for Cumbernauld, and came back to Celtic playing under the aforementioned Stein and captain Billy McNeill. Dalglish was part of the Celtic side going for nine league titles in a row.

In 1971/72 Dalglish established himself in the first team, scoring 23 league and cup goals in 49 games. He followed that up by becoming prolific for the Hoops, and was captain by 1975. By August of 1977, after making 320 appearances and scoring 167 goals, Kenny Dalglish signed for Liverpool for a record British transfer fee at the time. His medal haul at the Glasgow giants was impressive: four Scottish First Division titles, four Scottish Cups and one Scottish League Cup.

While Kenny wasn't a like-for-like replacement for recently departed Kevin Keegan, who had gone to Hamburg, he was able to take the number 7 shirt. Kenny scored on his Anfield debut against Newcastle, and scored the sixth and final goal against Hamburg in the second leg of the 1977 UEFA Super Cup Final. He was able to replace the all-world Keegan by making 61 appearances with 31 goals, and by scoring the game-winning goal in the 1978 European Cup Final.

He didn't stop there. The following year, he hit 21 league goals and established himself as an iron man. He played every league game for Liverpool well into the 1980/81 campaign. That year, Liverpool finished fifth in the league but still won the European Cup and the League Cup. During the 1982 season, Kenny regained his goalscoring form, scoring 13 times, as Liverpool won the league for the third time since Kenny had come down from Celtic.

Dalglish always had great players alongside him: the aforementioned Graeme Souness, Peter Beardsley, Ray Houghton, John Barnes and John Aldridge. His time as a Liverpool player was his most successful stretch. With him deployed as the club's number 7, Liverpool continued their ascension and domination of British and European club football. Liverpool were on a different level, and the supporters viewed Dalglish as their leader. This was when he got the title King Kenny, which he used until he was knighted.

Dalglish's tale extends beyond his club accomplishments: he was a national symbol for Scotland and Scottish football. In 102 appearances, which made him the most-capped player, he also scored 30 goals to share top spot overall with Denis Law. He wasn't known worldwide, maybe due to the fact that the Scottish national team were not well liked outside of the United Kingdom borders. Kenny became a wonderful manager in all his stops after his playing days were over. He did keep playing for a bit during his first spell in charge of Liverpool.

For all the great he did and continues to do, Kenny has watched in horror through many of the football disasters of the 70s and 80s. As a boy, he barely escaped the second Ibrox Stadium disaster in the 1970s. Then, as the crumbling of football stadiums in the 80s commenced, he watched as a player during the Heysel tragedy. That would be enough for most people to kick on, but as a manager he also saw the Hillsborough tragedy happen. Throughout it all, we can say Kenny is a good man, because he attended all 96 funerals of the victims of Hillsborough. This is what drove him from Liverpool the first time, as the weight of the city, managing and all the disasters took their toll on him.

As mentioned above, Liverpool and Flamengo met in Tokyo because they each won their continental cup. The Intercontinental Cup rotated between South American clubs and European sides winning it for the world title. Liverpool were feared around the world, kind of like Flamengo were in their domestic league. Liverpool were considered the favourites for the match but they had not seen as many expressive players on the pitch at the same time before. Zico was the top player in South America and this was his coming-out party in Europe.

Liverpool lined up in their normal 4-4-2 formation: Grobbelaar, Neal, Thompson, Hansen, Lawrenson, Lee, McDermott, Souness, Kennedy, Dalglish and Johnston. Flamengo lined up in a 4-3-3: Raul, Leandro, Marinho, Mozer, Júnior, Andrade, Adílio, Zico, Tita, Nunes and Lico.

Even with all the talent on the field, there was a nonchalant feeling in the stadium among the supporters, all 60,000 of them reported in attendance at Tokyo's national stadium. Liverpool were known for their scoring, so for the Brazilian giants to keep them out was a big surprise and a feather in the cap of Flamengo. Liverpool were kept off the scoreboard as Flamengo played brilliant football.

In the first half, Nunes scored two goals, a chip after a typically beautiful pass and the second coming off his right foot following a typical Flamengo move with several passes. Nunes's two goals in the first half were bracketed around Adílio's goal, after a fumble in the Liverpool box. Remember talking about Liverpool's defence having issues adjusting to Grobbelaar? That's where this came in. This sunk the English elite and European champions.

Zico was so good in the match that Souness couldn't even foul him. Souness made a career of hard play. He could stick a boot in on anyone. While he wasn't the quickest, he would get you. However, Zico wasn't one of Souness's victims. Liverpool manager Bob Paisley was always one to give credit where credit was due, saying in the aftermath of the match that Liverpool were beaten by the better side. But he wasn't the only one talking about the Brazilians. Ray Kennedy didn't want to have to face them again. To understand why this was so big, you have to comprehend what Liverpool were during this time.

This was the height of Liverpool's powers. Bob Paisley was still manager and Kenny Dalglish et al were there too. This was also the last time when Aston Villa were considered a force, challenging the Reds strongly on many occasions. In that respect, the 1970s was a fun decade for the First Division – Derby County won a couple of league titles and Aston Villa and Nottingham Forest reigned supreme in Europe. Fergie was still in Scotland too, and just the year before had won the European Cup Winners' Cup with Aberdeen. This, of course, was in a time when the game wasn't dominated by money like it is today.

That's not saying there wasn't money in the sport; Liverpool were able to sign up some new additions. Players came into the side such as Bruce Grobbelaar, Mark Lawrenson, Ian Rush, Craig Johnston and Ronnie Whelan, and they'd all be key to the success of the 80s, some of which we talked about above.

The road to the Intercontinental Cup first had to go through the European Cup. In 1981/82, Liverpool entered five competitions, reaching the quarter-final of the European Cup, but losing against CSKA Sofia 2-1, and bowing out of the FA Cup in the fifth round, but winning the League Cup following a 3-1 win over Spurs and winning the league title alongside that too. The success, overall, continued to come in.

Liverpool didn't take the Club World Cup seriously; it was a rushed match in December which was a potential disruption to their domestic title push. Liverpool were winning league titles like Manchester United did in the 90s and the early part of the 2000s, so for a cup competition to potentially derail their domestic dominance was not an option to explore any further or, essentially, risk. It would have gone against everything Bill Shankly had preached. This was until the opportunity to play Brazilian giants Flamengo arose.

Because of this boycott, there was a desperate need for change, which came in 1980 when Toyota stepped in to sponsor the competition. This moved the match to be played on neutral ground in Tokyo. It also became a one-off final, after being a two-legged final for the majority of its existence. Also added was the Falklands War and, as covered very well by many historians, Boca Juniors had been impacted by this. Read my last book about Boca Juniors to see that story.

English clubs, including Liverpool, started making their way back into the fold, but were soundly beaten each time. When Nottingham Forest finally played, they were beaten, and then Liverpool as we saw above and Aston Villa a year later. There was a duelling problem here with the British clubs, South America, the Falklands War and British Prime Minister Margaret Thatcher.

Chapter 7

Thatcher Hated the Sport

ONE OF the reasons this win was big for Flamengo was the tenor of football back in Britain. The 70s and 80s in the United Kingdom were bad for stadiums; there were more than a dozen disasters on the homeland. This doesn't include, in the mid-80s, the Heysel disaster. Some of this was due to hooliganism, but the government tried to write it all off as the fault of the fans. However, any person with common sense would know that the government and the police force pointed the finger to deal with it.

The British establishment have always viewed the football fan as scum, as was shown early in the book. Flamengo were built among the 'low class'. The establishment in Britain viewed their supporters as uneducated, anti-social young men who got their jollies off of kicking people and destruction upon whoever they saw. To be fair, it was not like the establishment came up with this all out of thin air. For the most part, this is what they saw on a weekly basis. This was a response to the turbulent 70s and the punk-rock scene.

Hillsborough, which happened at the end of the 80s, showed the extent to which the ruling class would go to justify their stereotype. Supporters were smeared, and the tabloid press didn't help. While all of this was unfounded, if you repeat a lie enough, and long enough, it becomes fact no matter how much you credibly deny it. There are many books, podcasts, documentaries and series about Hillsborough that can do it more of a service. The footage and images from the disasters around the time prove that the fans needed it. This was Margaret Thatcher's Britain, and it was obvious to anyone what her opinion of the average football fan was; her attitude was very similar to the miners' situation. Her views were ignorant, ill-informed but deeply entrenched. They were all based on the thought that the unwashed masses are the enemy within.

The sport and the terraces were very different at the time. If you want a general feel of the game, take a look at the stadiums in South America pre- and post-pandemic. The stadiums were primitive, and as there was a lack of toilets for both sexes, you wouldn't see many, if any, women fans at matches. The away ends had a concentration camp look as fans were corralled in cages with wire-mesh fences. Basically, it was dehumanising, and you could see why it turned into hooliganism.

Most of this is gone as money went into the sport, and part of the change was due to football revolutionising in spite of Thatcher's negative policies. She created a 'war cabinet' on football hooligans, making ideas like banning fans from travelling to away matches and having to carry ID cards. Sounds very similar to other totalitarianism ideas. As these ideas kept rolling in, it took the fun out of the sport, when it was needed.

The changes to the game after Thatcher was out of office were brought about by the Taylor Report. Lord Justice Taylor's Report helped usher these in after the Hillsborough disaster. It was a huge indictment on how the sport was being run. Lord Justice Taylor showed that fencing people in like animals would create more problems. If you treated people with respect, then they would behave well; if you built stadiums in a fan-friendly way, the game would improve. And for the most part, from the 90s on, that's what you saw. There hasn't been a disaster since, because the Report showed it wasn't the fans' fault.

For as bad as Thatcher and the Tory government were, and to a point have been for mainland Britain, it has been worse for Liverpool. The phrase 'Scouse not English' is apt, which manifests itself in the fact that Liverpool fans also boo 'God Save the Queen'. Liverpool is a large port and was, until the government strangled the docks, one of the great ports of the British Empire. The area was also settled by the Irish, and still identifies as Irish in some respects. Thatcher also, during the Toxteth riots, was urged to abandon Liverpool, or manage its decline with her chancellor, Geoffrey Howe.

As we mentioned with the Lord Taylor Report, cage people enough and they will rebel. In that vein, the constant pain the national government were inflicting on Liverpool manifested itself on the city council, in a Trotskyist group called Militant. They took control of the city council in the 80s, and there were some dissenting views also. Simon Hughes wrote a great book on this, *There She Goes: Liverpool, A City on its Own: The Long Decade: 1979–1993*.

One part of his book which talked about the managed decline stated: 'I don't think people really realized what this meant, it meant if you were struggling, you were doomed essentially, which in the framework of the Conservative government'. There's the major difference between the Liberals/Labour and the Tories: the Liberals want to help everyone, down to the poor. The Tory government were looking for the best and brightest, ignoring any way they could help anyone struggling. That included immigrants, the Irish and the black community. There was also massive unemployment.

Another huge problem during this time period for the UK was the police force. All over the land, the police and special forces were being used on home soil to harass the citizens. Northern Ireland was a war zone, and no matter what people did in Liverpool, the police were after you. At football, they were after the supporters. Hillsborough showed the failings of the police force in the country many times over.

So with all this bad going on, the football was a relief from this. Liverpool FC weren't the only great club during this time; Howard Kendall's Everton were right up there, if not better, during this period. Many people talk about how great the Merseyside derby is, and one of its heydays was during the 80s. You could see the escapism from the day-to-day lives of the citizens.

The government were only facing the supporters of the teams, not the clubs funding the supporters. Christopher Hylland's book *Tears at La Bombonera* talks about the difference between the South American *barra brava* and British groups: 'The British football firms, of the 1970s and 1980s, may have been organized to an extent, but they didn't have access to the club like the barra brava do.' Thatcher was only going after the fans, and the punishment would be on the clubs for the actions. The barra brava are part of the fabric of the sport in South America, even at this time. They want to curry favour with a club; the hooligans were, in their minds, defending a club from the other fans on their own merit.

Thatcher was bad for the rest of the country as well as Liverpool. She spent most of 1984 battling the miners during the coal strike. She was dismantling the coal industry but taking her time with it. Granted, it was almost four years after the 1981 match, but Thatcher had been in government since the 70s.

History has shown that the first five months of 1985 were among the worst for the national game. Between the Luton Town riot, the Valley Parade fire and Heysel, the sport was trying to reinvent itself.

The upper crust of society, who never liked football from the beginning, were questioning the future of the sport. It was more of a mindset than the trouble in the sport. They were not completely wrong; by the 1983/84 season, attendances were falling, and Aston Villa, who had won the European Cup in the early 80s, were down also.

This was also the decade when society was very run down, with unemployment and riots. So when leagues reached the end of the terrible 1985 season, Thatcher wanted to end hooliganism. Spoiler alert: even though the sport has calmed down, they are still about. Her rules, set out on April Fool's Day of 1985, included ID cards, better fencing and closed-circuit television. Clubs had to follow what Downing Street said, and this was all before the Bradford City fire on 11 May.

The same day at St Andrew's, Birmingham City's home, a wall collapsed as Birmingham fans clashed with Leeds supporters, causing the death of a young supporter. The Prime Minister ignored the obvious bad decision to hold the European Cup Final at an old, crumbling stadium, Heysel, and blamed the Liverpool fans, possibly a forerunner to the blaming of Liverpool fans for Hillsborough. Thatcher and the sport's governing bodies immediately withdrew English clubs from European competition.

The fans did not sit there idly – they fought back as the Football Supporters' Association (FSA)[31] was formed by a group of fans in a Merseyside pub. This brought the game back to the fans, since there was a need for a democratic, national organisation to campaign on behalf of them. Not all fans were hooligans, as the opinion of society was towards them. Also, it brought in the explosion of football fanzines, which has shown that fans were not stupid, but funny and creative.

The FSA, at times, stood up for the victims of these disasters, while also opposing the government's identity-card proposal. However, despite the successes, the FSA have never had a massive membership, even with the huge fan power out there. They were also powerless to stop the requirement of all-seater stadiums after the Taylor Report. Another issue they have not got a hold of is the massive ticket-price increase that has taken out a whole class of supporters from stadiums.

The FSA also gave the opposition to Thatcher that was so lacking in Westminster, but it was far too late for the self-imposed ban on English teams. It was quickly ratified by UEFA and kept in place until 1990, when many attempts of a breakaway league were started by the biggest clubs. Eventually, years later, English clubs came back into Europe, even though Liverpool had to wait longer to get back.

---

31 www.wsc.co.uk/the-archive/100-Fan-culture/1469-the-past-imperfect

Chapter 8

Life in Rio

ONCE YOU have seen the mindset and the problems behind Liverpool at the time, you can understand how deflating a loss is. This is an oversimplification of feelings, because while football clubs want to win everything, the Intercontinental Cup wasn't a big thing. Liverpool won the rematch with Flamengo in the now-named Club World Cup in 2020, but that was the one medal that got away from the dominant era. We need to show what it was like for the fans in Rio.

As with anything in Brazil, there is always a show, and making people feel good is at their core. South America is unstable to say the least. There has been a military presence on the streets, but they are cool to the local residents.[32] Most people who come to Rio de Janeiro live a normal life, moving about the city's districts very easily.

Rio is nicknamed *a cidade maravilhosa* – the marvellous city – and from the backdrop, you can see that in any picture you take. It's also known throughout the world as a beach city, and Rio also has the world's largest urban forest in the

---

32 https://www.goodschoolsguide.co.uk/international/brazil/rio-de-janeiro/expat-guide

Tijuca Forest. High above all of that on the Corcovado peak of the *Pão de Açúcar* – Sugarloaf Mountain – is the world-famous *Cristo Redentor* (Christ the Redeemer), a 98ft statue of Jesus with arms outstretched over the city.

Rio is loosely divided into four districts: *centro*, the *Zona Sul* (South Zone), the *Zona Oeste* (West Zone) and the *Zona Norte* (North Zone). Centro, as you can tell, is the heart of the city, where you will find old and new Rio living happily side by side. You will find narrow streets, baroque churches and grand architecture juxtaposed with modern structures. The port, which has sustained the city for its existence, is also part of this zone. Very few people live in this part of the city.

In the Western Zone, Barra da Tijuca is a popular choice for people when it comes to housing. It has been called the Miami of the South, as the architecture and life looks like South Beach. What makes this part so attractive is the space and security, as families can rent space with gardens and pools. It's generally a safer place to live in. There are also British and American schools there. As you go further north, people of lower incomes are more featured.

Rio has a bad reputation, but that's par for the course for most of South America. As mentioned above, the military has been known to roam the streets, but the amount of ordinary street crime is the most you are likely to encounter. You have to make sure you don't wear jewellery or watches, and keep cameras and mobiles out of sight. More importantly, do not speak English loudly, because criminals prey on tourists. If you are challenged in a fight, always hand over your stuff right away. That being said, most expatriates live a normal life.

Rio is a steamy, tropical city, apropos of what you would expect. Summer for South America is December through to

March, and it's the stickiest time of the year. There's also a lot of rain. Air conditioning is commonplace in Rio, but for homeowners, it's basically in your bedroom. It can get cold in the winter but it is not like Glasgow or London. Because of such a climate, it is good for asthma sufferers, and you can see people moving there for relief.

The natives of Rio are called *Cariocas* and there are a lot of them. Rio is the second-biggest city in Brazil just after São Paulo. Many of the people are migrants to the city, living in *favelas*, the sprawling shanty towns that have brought Rio bad press recently. These shanty towns are very dangerous places, and no foreigner should enter. They are controlled by drug traffickers who have their own sense of discipline.

Rio's geography means that not much physically separates the rich from the poor. These shanty towns are sometimes right next to the prosperous districts and new buildings. Due to the COVID pandemic, these shanty towns have grown, along with the number of homeless people.

Despite all of this, Cariocas are very easy to get along with. However, like with many things Brazilian, timekeeping and punctuality are not their strong points. It's quite normal for Brazilians to arrive at an event two hours or more later than a specific time on an invitation. Famously, Pelé did the same thing in New York City when he had his arrival press conference for the New York Cosmos.

It is essential for people living in Brazil to learn Portuguese just to survive. Brazilians do know a little English, but it's hard to find anyone in Rio who can communicate easily in anything other than Portuguese. Most expatriates learn Portuguese, either in a school or one-on-one training. Most big businesses pay for their employees to receive language studies.

Brazil is the world's largest Roman Catholic country, but the Church does not have a massive hold on the country as one would expect. Many aren't practising Catholics. The reason for the hold not being that strong is the rising participation of evangelical Protestantism, which is around 20 per cent. These Protestants are very active across the country, and are growing rapidly, particularly in the poor areas. The English-speaking community in Rio is served by the Anglican Church, the Christ Church and the Roman Catholic Church, which are all in the southern part of Botafogo. Then to add another layer to this, some of the natives follow traditional Afro-Brazilian religions such as *Candomblé*, *Macumba* and *Umbanda*, which have very similar traits to voodoo. They involve worshipping a wide variety of idols, making food sacrifices and dance/trance rituals. Brazilians are generally superstitious.

Transportation in the city was transformed with the run-up to the Rio Olympics. There is the Rio Metro, a rapid transit system, along with tram services. The Metro runs out to Barra da Tijuca, which cuts journey times. Cars are also a big form of transportation in the city, and the easy-going natives become aggressive, and lack courtesy and patience when driving. No quarter is given to anyone, and obeying the traffic lights is viewed as being optional. Lane discipline isn't practised in Rio either, and roundabouts aren't a normal thing in the city. The main roads are in a very bad state, and, generally, 40,000 people die on Brazil's roads every year.

After six months, expatriates have to apply for a Brazilian licence. Most nationals of English-speaking countries need to only register photos and fingerprints with the federal police. Then they just have to undergo a psychological test and a basic medical exam. The psychological test is basically about your dreams for the future and filling in puzzles. Some people from European countries have to do a driving test. Owning a car isn't a necessity; people can walk and use public transport if needed.

Brazil is a struggling country financially, and money for resources that better society or people isn't there. Public health services in Rio are very poor; however, private facilities are very good. Major city hospitals have some of the best trauma teams in the region. Healthcare in the private sector is very good, generally equal to what is available to people around the world.

People are able to choose their own doctors and healthcare professionals. Many doctors speak English and have completed their medical studies in the USA. Expats have their babies in Rio, and those children get their Brazilian citizenship right away. Cosmetic surgery is a big business in Rio, as most Brazilians have a nip or a tuck. There are plenty of good dentists in Rio, and again they do cosmetic procedures, and it's not cheap.

Being a large city, Rio has restaurants that serve all types of cuisine. The traditional Brazilian food is everywhere: this includes black beans and rice, with roast meat, vegetables and flour. Seafood is very good, since Rio is a port city. Brazilians traditionally eat their main meal at lunchtime, so lunch hours are long. They do have their alcoholic drinks too; the beer is good, and refreshing in the hot climate. The wine is improving, and other South American wines are very available.

Shopping is expensive in Rio if imported. Lego tends to be four times the price it is elsewhere. Clothing usually uses the continental, European-sizing system, while Brazil has its own shoe sizing. Decent clothes for tall people are very hard to find in Rio. The market, or the grocery store, has got much better with time. Most food is grown in the country and able to be bought at reasonable prices.

Not everything in Rio has been great; dealing with the Maracanã has been a thorn in the side of many people. It was turned over to the government of the State of Rio de Janeiro in 1974; after the states of Guanabara and Rio de Janeiro were merged, the responsible entity for the stadium was the State. The merger was to balance political power between the economically poor of the State of Rio and the powerful of the city of Rio, as it was a federal district from 1960. Thus, the owner of the Maracanã from 1974 to 2014 was the government of the State of Rio de Janeiro.

In 2013, the Maracanã was sold to a new controlling company, with the negotiation process between the clubs and a consortium led by Odebrecht. This was the same company that opened a stadium, Engenhão, in 2007 for the Pan-American Games. There was a structural failure in the roof of the stadium, but no one was prosecuted for this, and serious financial losses were suffered by the clubs of Rio de Janeiro, with the largest being at Botafogo.

When the negotiation started between the clubs and the consortium, there was only one bidder, ironically from the city. The city was going to give the Maracanã to Flamengo, because it had the proverbial knife to the neck of the people who needed it the most. It did not go through a vote in the club's internal councils as required by the by-laws of each club. This was in keeping with the traditional lack of ethics, morals and principles of the Brazilian political system, to get at the money of Flamengo.

In 2017, the governor of Rio de Janeiro, who renovated and provided the previous deal, Sérgio Cabral Filho, was put in prison. The executives of Odebrecht and the public accountants who did the bidding were arrested. Making it even worse, the Federal Public Ministry requested and the Superior Court of Justice ordered the arrest of five councillors of the Court of Auditors of Rio de Janeiro. This was a big problem, and the unfolding of 'Operation Lava Jato'.

The directors were accused of receiving bribes from Odebrecht according to company executives. To add more insult to injury, the president of TCE-Rio, Jonas Lopes, asked for money for the approval of the Maracanã concession notice for six years. The court put aside 21 of the 22 investigations of the stadium. With all of this hanging above their heads, the public realised that the bidding process needed to be reopened. However, the powers that be wanted to not make official statements and hoped the revolting voices kept quiet so the corruption could win over.

The government, again trying to use Flamengo, wanted to trap them into being forced from the Maracanã. It was also trying to force the concession to French company Lagardère, with the Flamengo board refusing to negotiate. The French acquisition was taken for granted, as league clubs with an arbitration held at CBF made it so that any club couldn't host games outside of their home state. During the 2016 Brazilian Championship, without the Maracanã, the club had to use stadiums in Brasília, São Paulo (the Pacaembu), Cuiabá, Natal, Florianópolis and Cariacica. So this hurt Flamengo, but it seems that was the point. In 2017 the board signed a contract for an initial three-year span, with a renewable option for three more years, to use the Estádio Luso Brasileiro, in Ilha do Governador, which was Portuguesa's home stadium. The losses by Flamengo to the public–private partnership were beyond financial; they were affecting the on-the-field and image value.

Finally, in May 2017, Flamengo and Rio de Janeiro, through Mayor Marcelo Crivella, were able to build a stadium for 25,000 fans in Gávea, ironically the day before the French company Lagardère withdrew their offer to take over the Maracanã. The state government, through back channels, kept talking about a new bid, with the clubs participating in a consortium that would take over the Maracanã, a move that would have stopped the fraudulent bids.

Between Flamengo's willingness to fight corruption and the state government taking their own time, this all took a while. On 6 September 2017, Flamengo announced the signing of an option for purchase of a plot of land between Avenida Brasil and Linda Vermelha with the option lasting for 120 days, so until 6 January. Economic feasibility studies would be carried out also.

It was the start of 2018 and the government of Rio continued to drag its feet, studying the conditions to launch another notice for the sale. The amount of studying the government was doing for a simple study, making it out to need great technical knowledge, was extreme – a kid in elementary school could figure this out. The number of millionaires around to help out with the case was another problem. What stadium alternatives did Flamengo have? Engenhão was out – so was São Januário due to a bad relationship with Vasco's board. Volta Redonda and Macaé would not provide a great financial return. A stadium of its own would take years to be ready, so Flamengo were up with their backs against the wall. Just what the authorities wanted. A buyer did come in to help, Consortium Maracanã, and they made a provisional agreement with each other at the end of 2013 for three years. There was a problem for Flamengo like usual, because they had no other stadium to play in. So they had to accept a share of the costs to be considered to play in the Maracanã, without having the ability to supervise these costs. The Consortium Maracanã then inflated the costs to reduce Flamengo's profit margins that should have gone to the club.

Flamengo's board of directors and its legal department were determined to take legal action against the preceding trouble it had had. They had moral, material, sporting and institutional damages they could recover. Flamengo lost revenue with inflation, and having to play in front of smaller audiences because of the unavailability of an honest agreement for use of the Maracanã. They had sporting losses as they had to play in different stadiums during the 2016 Brazilian Championship, which probably cost them the national title. The revenue losses stemmed from money being kept from ticket offices and the Supporter Partner Programme. Legal action was for damages against Odebrecht, and Botafogo as well as public entities for the successive financial crimes.

Chapter 9

The Drought

HISTORIC YEARS are usually hard to follow up. Flamengo's 1981 season was one for the ages, and the record books. The club was put together very well, so needless to say, they could continue the success. As mentioned earlier, a year of play for Brazilian clubs is a slog and 1982 was a World Cup year. This was Brazil coming off a record era for the national team. As we know, Zico left and came back to Flamengo, but some of the other players had to go also.

On the club side, Flamengo did not follow up their historic year with a repeat of the previous season, but they did win the country league like normal in those days – Zico got the most goals in the league. That was par for the course at that time, but the Copa Libertadores was a different story. Flamengo made it to the semi-finals before losing out 1-0 to Peñarol on 16 November 1982. A Libertadores mainstay won the title for the first time since the 70s.

On 25 April 1982, Flamengo beat Grêmio with a goal from Nunes near the start of the match, for the Brazilian Championship for the second time. This made them the holders of all the competitions they played in at the time: the Guanabara Cup, the Intercontinental Cup, the Rio State Cup, the Brazilian Championship and the

Libertadores. Then the tear-down started; the titles were the first to go.

In the second half of 1982, the club won the Guanabara Cup for the fifth consecutive year. Then the wear and tear of the endless matches took their toll. On 5 December 1982 Vasco beat Flamengo 1-0 with a goal by Marquinho to win the State title. Fifteen days later, club president Domingo Bosco died which, as brought up later, ruined the squad.

In January of 1983, Flamengo sent Tita away on loan to Grêmio for Baltazar, marking the first of the great team to leave. By the end of February, Nunes had left for Botafogo on loan after a disagreement with Carpegiani. Nunes was approached by Palmeiras, Ponte Preta, New York Cosmos and Millonarios before going to Botafogo.

March was an open door for the club, as Andrade and Lico were lost due to knee problems. Carpegiani left after 20 months and many cups while in charge, for a big contract with Al-Nassr. By the end of May, only six starters from Tokyo were still around: Raul, Leandro, Marinho, Júnior, Adílio and Zico. And Zico did not last too much longer at the club, as he was off to Udinese at the start of June. The fans, the club and even Flamengo president Antônio Augusto Dunshee de Abranches were all depressed by the legend leaving for Italy. Ten days later, Zico came back as an opponent with Udinese for a couple of minutes in a 4-2 win for the Italians. By the end of the year in 1983, 39-year-old goalkeeper Raul had also left the team. In his place came River Plate legend Ubaldo Fillol, a World Cup winner with Argentina.

In another shocking transfer for Flamengo fans, on 15 June 1984 Júnior was sold to Torino. By this time, only Mozer, Adílio and Andrade were left from the Tokyo team.

Then by the summer of 1987, Adílio was the only one left, as Mozer was sold to Benfica in June of that year. Adílio would not last the season at the club, as he was signed by Coritiba on 9 September 1987 to compete in the new Brazilian Championship, Copa União.

After hitting the top in a two-year cycle, 1983 was always going to be a hard time for the club. In April of 1983 the club was in crisis. They seemed to be living on the other side of the coin, as they were eliminated from the Copa Libertadores by Peñarol in the Maracanã in November of the previous year. Then December got worse when they lost the Rio title to Vasco, and Domingo Bosco, the president, died of a cerebral thrombosis. Without Bosco to steady the ship, friction set into the club. Tita and Nunes fought with coach Carpegiani and left the club for loans with Grêmio and Botafogo respectively. Next, the coach had it out with physical trainer José Roberto Francalacci, who had been with the club for 12 years. Francalacci was sacked. Carpegiani, who was under pressure as well, was sacked after 12 matches.

It could have been another great season for the club in 1983, but it is one of the most underappreciated seasons ever. It's also the Campeonato Brasil title which is the least talked about among the six. The first in 1980 kicked off the golden era, the second in 1982 was the anointing of the great side, 1987 had legal controversies, 1992 was the year of 'Gaúcho's Boys' and 2009 was the great journey of Adriano and Petković; 1983 kept the good times rolling. The 3-0 victory over Santos on 29 May 1983 only kept Zico and Adílio in the middle of the starting line-up from the glory years. It was also the year that Zico left for the time being to Italy. On top of that, the cup came under the direction of a manager who wasn't Flamengo born and bred. Until the end of September, Flamengo lived a flawless 1982.

Despite all the cup winnings, the club still had not contested the Guanabara Cup of 1982. That was seen to with a goal from Adílio in a 1-0 win over Vasco, which was the fifth year in a row winning the Guanabara Cup. In those last three months of 1982, there was the Taça Rio, the Copa Libertadores and the final round of the Carioca. Flamengo did bring in new players in Wilsinho and Zezé.

On 19 October, Flamengo were in Montevideo for their debut in the Libertadores against Peñarol. This would be a big two-legged affair anyway, as the Uruguayan side were one of the major clubs in Libertadores history. Unfortunately, Flamengo lost 1-0 with a goal from Ernesto Vargas. So the return was going to be a very traumatic match. Between the two legs, Flamengo won at River Plate 3-1 at Monumental de Núñez and 4-2 at the Maracanã.

When the second leg took place on 16 November, Flamengo played horribly. Brazilian Jair scored to beat Flamengo 1-0, sending the holders out of the cup. Three weeks later, Flamengo lost the Rio title to Vasco. Not the best way to continue the great times. What was up with Flamengo? In São Paulo, however, supporters and the like were happy to see this all come crumbling down. Clêber Camerino directed the squad in a goalless draw with Guarani in Campinas. Flamengo looked for another manager, asking Evaristo to come in, but stuck with former player Carlos Alberto Torres. He had, in September 1982, played a friendly with the New York Cosmos versus Flamengo. Carlos Alberto, despite being a legendary centre-half, built his team around a more combative midfield. The idea was to take advantage of the vim and vigour of Elder and Júlio

César Barbosa, with Vitor as the destroyer in the midfield. This would allow Adílio and Zico to create, getting the ball up top to Baltazar.

This worked, as Flamengo beat Corinthians 5-1, as de Leão, Zenon and Sócrates had goals called back by the referee. Flamengo then drew 1-1 with Goiás, and a 2-0 win over Guarani put them through to the quarter-finals of the Carioca with Corinthians and Guarani. The Vasco matches, like most years, were ones to write home about. On a Thursday night, Flamengo dominated the play, and a move between Zico, Júnior and Adílio resulted in a goal off the foot of Adílio in the first half. In the second half, a rather choppy part of the match, the winning goal on the 23rd-minute mark was scored by Júlio César. He took it from a great cross from the right side by Marinho, and sneaked it past a misguided Vasco. All was not safe for Flamengo as they could still lose in the return leg.

On the Sunday, Vasco started out ahead with a lucky break by Roberto rolling a free kick to Eloi, who put it past Raul. Little by little, Flamengo regained control of the match even though down a goal. They did waste time on the ball, and as the clock approached the end of the match, Elder sent a ball into Adílio, who headed it into the box and Zico put the ball in the back of the net. Vasco turned to the referee, because they said Zico was well offside. Roberto tried to attack referee Valquir Pimentel, and was expelled while being escorted from the pitch. Antônio Lopes tried to accuse Flamengo of playing poorly.

What mattered in the long run was Flamengo were in the semi-finals, and facing Athletico Paranaense, who had just beaten tournament favourites São Paulo. Even with Raul being injured, Flamengo poured on the goals:

headers by Zico and Júlio César, a normal goal by Vitor and Zico's penalty kick. But in the second leg, it started off very differently. Flamengo had two clear chances for Baltazar saved, only to see Washington score his brace. Either way, Flamengo were through to the final of the Campeonato Brasileiro.

Up next was the final against Santos, and by being in the final, Flamengo had confirmed their place in the 1984 Libertadores. It did not start out so well for Flamengo: Elder was close to the goal and fumbled, as Pita eventually got it and scored for Santos. At half-time, Carlos Alberto switched Júlio César for Bebeto. Another blunder in the second half, when Flamengo complained for a foul, let Serginho get a hold of the ball and put it in the back of the net. During the goal celebration, he was hit by a firecracker and had to be assisted off the field. After the distraction, Júnior took a corner to Mozer, who passed it to Baltazar for a goal. This kept Flamengo alive in the championship.

With the 2-1 defeat out of the way, in the second leg Flamengo needed two goals to take the title. If it was a one-goal difference, the match would go to extra time, and then penalties for the decision. In the first minutes of the match, Zico scored the first goal Flamengo needed. Baltazar missed a great chance for the second goal on five minutes, putting the ball over the top of the goal. Next, the referee let Toninho Silva foul Zico in the area, and nothing was called. Moments later, Pita was stopped by Marinho close to the area, but nothing was doing either.

Santos gained control, and made enough moves up the other end to scare Flamengo. Finally, there was a foul near the line for Flamengo; Zico took the free kick, sending it into Leandro for the 2-0 score that Flamengo needed for the win. This was all in the first half.

In the second half,, Santos played with an urgency to get the match back on their side. Flamengo would have none of that, especially Adílio. He was ever present in the run to the championship. Adílio was the complete box-to-box midfielder, this being one of the best matches of his career. He also confirmed the title for Flamengo, scoring near the end of the match, on 89 minutes; the third title, capping off another great year, and a managing title for Carlos Alberto. Then the cracks in the foundation started to show.

Carlinhos was the next manager up and still can't snap the disastrous campaign. In the Libertadores, Flamengo drew with Blooming 0-0 and they lost 3-1 to Bolívar. Then they came back to the Rio tournament and were eliminated, which meant Carlinhos was sacked. His assistant Cleber Camerino took charge of one match with Guarani, a goalless draw in Campinas. The press in São Paulo were gloating that the great era was over for Flamengo.

São Paulo were just waiting for their turn at the top, as a club from São Paulo had not won the cup since 1978. In the third round of the national tournament, São Paulo de Careca entered with the best defence and one of the best attacks in the country. Palmeiras brought in Batista from Grêmio, and manager Rubens Minelli was always in the running for the Seleção job. Minelli had beaten Flamengo in the previous round 3-1 at Morumbi. Santos had their best team since the Pelé era, and Corinthians were the State champions.

Among the great Cariocas, Fluminense and Botafogo were there in the third round like normal. Vasco, a thorn in the side of Flamengo, had qualified by drawing with Bahia in the Maracanã. América, a good team, were coached by Zico's brother Edu Antunes. The key to growth in the tournament for Flamengo was another new manager. This time it was former Seleção captain and New York Cosmos defender Carlos Alberto Torres. He had just hung up his boots, so he was new to the managerial occupation. Carlos was inspired by the Corinthian Democracy that was in force at Corinthians, the next opponents on 17 April. There weren't any new tactical changes; all Carlos asked was for Elder and Júlio César to do the work so that Zico and Adílio had the freedom to make moves towards the goal.

Corinthians came into the match with the absences of Casagrande, Biro-Biro, Ataliba and Paulinho. Flamengo, for their part, were without the services of Andrade, Robertinho and Lico, who was out for the season with knee surgery. Even with all of this, there was still some pain Flamengo had to suffer during the match. On the 15-minute mark, Flamengo had a goal disallowed after Adílio hit a rebound after Mozer's shot.

Corinthians got into the game around the 23rd minute with a corner kick from Paulo Egídio; Sócrates aimed for goal but Júnior got in the way. In the 28th minute Mozer fouled Vidotti near the area, giving Zenon a free kick that hit the crossbar. Flamengo's response was immediate while being pushed on by the fans. Júlio César found Zico with a pass, who headed it to Leão for a 1-0 lead. That just got Flamengo going, and in the second half they went for more.

Baltazar put them ahead 2-0 with a header. By the end of the match Flamengo had romped to a 5-1 win, and the uncomplicated nature of how Carlos Alberto managed the match stopped the bad times. On the same day, São Paulo went to Porto Alegre and were demolished by the same 5-1 scoreline, to Grêmio.

171

Having a great club in South America also means that players get poached by European clubs. Pelé was one of only a handful of South American players who never played in Europe. It was only a matter of time that Zico would move to Europe, and finally, on 2 June 1983, Flamengo president Antônio Augusto Dunshee de Abranches announced the sale of Zico to Udinese. Eventually, Zico did come back for a friendly with Udinese, but the star had finally left for overseas.

Zico's transfer was not the easiest either in Italy. And it wasn't the first time Italians had come looking for Zico. The first rumours of Zico leaving Flamengo started in 1980, and if he had have moved, this book would not have happened. Zico at Milan would be a fun thought, and not many people would have to change colours, since Milan wear basically the same design. In March of 1980, as part of the Totonero scandal, Milan were one of seven clubs relegated to Serie B for match-fixing. Also in this scandal was Italian national team player Paolo Rossi, who was banned for three years originally but reduced to two years. Ironically, Paolo Rossi played some friendlies in indoor soccer in America during this time.

In 1981, Massimo Giacomini wanted to bring the Brazilian in, after bringing Milan back to Serie A. Rossoneri vice-president Gianni Rivera wanted to push the button for Zico. Basically, Milan were offering the player a good salary, but wouldn't pay a cent to Flamengo. This angered the Brazilian club, and Zico. Supporters did not want to see Zico go either. Milan made offers to Flamengo until 31 May 1981. At that point, Zico's contract was renewed, and the great times of 1981 happened.

Milan at the time also went in for Belgian Jan Ceulemans, who was at Club Brugge. Just like Zico, the

Belgian rejected the Italian giants. A third player was also looked at, which was Hans Krankl, who chose Barcelona instead, who had Diego Maradona. So after all of this, the club was only able to get Joe Jordan, albeit a very good player. But Jordan was 30 and on the downside of his career.

As we know, Zico did show up in Italy, but for a much smaller club, Udinese. After the massive 1982 World Cup failure of the Brazilian national team, the sporting director of Udinese, Franco Dal Cin, offered up a deal, with Udinese paying half the cash, and a company who would have the rights to his image would pay the rest. The big money coming in helped Flamengo, because Brazil was going through a difficult time economically.

Ironically, one of the great matches in Zico's time in Italy was a match on 8 January 1984 at the San Siro against Milan which ended in a 3-3 tie. Zico scored an amazing overhead kick, which could be considered one of the best of his career. The Brazilian great was greeted at the San Siro with great affection by the Rossoneri fans. Former Watford striker Luther Blissett, another one of the players who came from the United Kingdom, missed a sitter in the match.

Zico's transfer at 30 years old to Udinese was not without its twists and turns. First, it had to go through the legal work to clear it. Luciano Lama was the general secretary of the Italian General Confederation of Labour, and Federico Sordillowho was a law student and former president of Milan in 1971/72 when they won the Italian Cup, and president of FIGC, the Italian football federation, needed to take a look at the transfer deal. All the parties were given a few days to conclude profitable contracts for everyone. Also at the time, Roma were completing the transfer from Atlético Mineiro of Toninho Cerezo, a defensive midfielder, so both transfers had to be scrutinised. Neither party suspected any controversy in the decisions because they figured it was an open and shut case.

To plead their cases, the mayor of Udine, Angelo Candolini, wanted the Minister of Tourism and Entertainment Nicola Signorello, Loris Fortuna, Minister for Civilian Protection, Giorgio Santuz, Undersecretary of the Treasury, Martino Scovacricchi, Undersecretary of Defence, and Francesco, to decide the solution to the transfers with the Italian Olympic Committee (CONI). Finally, on Saturday, 9 July, the CONI rejected the transfers because Grouping Ltd, who were going to pay half the transfers because they owned the rights to the images, were a shell company. The CONI had a point; Grouping Ltd were not registered on any list, and there was no known address, just a church. However, to get both over the line, a council of three people, Massimo Severo, Giuseppe Guarino and Raario Nicolo, came back with a verdict allowing the transfers to go through.

Zico leaving caused a split in the board. President Dunshee de Abranches resigned in anger. The split was between two political groups, one led by Marcio Braga and the other by George Helal. These two groups succeeded each other in the next four elections. The winner of the 1983 election was George Helal for his term of 1984–86, his vice-president of football was Josef Berensztein, and Isaias Tinoco was the manager. In the following election, Marcio Braga, 1987/88, was elected president, and Tinoco left for Vasco, being replaced by Luiz Henrique de Menezes.

To add to the confusion, for the 1989/90 season the president was Gilberto Cardoso Filho, with George Helal as vice-president of football and Josef Berensztein as vice-president of finance. By the start of 1990, the club wanted a revolution, and they attempted it by hiring Francisco Horta as executive manager. Horta had been the president of Fluminense from 1975 to 1977, and he revolutionised the football market by setting up Maquina Tricolor, winning 23 matches, drawing seven and losing only two, with 74 goals and only 26 conceded. The key was hiring Domingos Bosco as a professional. Managers at that point were not professional, or paid. However, Marcio Braga, the president, was brought back between 1977 and 1980. During this time period, the club won their first Brazilian title, which laid the groundwork for the national titles of 1982 and 1983, and the Libertadores and Intercontinental Cup of 1981. When he returned in 1987, the club won the Brazilian title, and he then came back a third time, and they won the Brazilian title in 1992.

The troubled second half of 1983 ended with a goal conceded in stoppage time scored by Assis while playing for Fluminense. The 1984 season was the fourth straight year in the Copa Libertadores, but there was a need for a squad refresh. Raul, at 39, hung up his goalkeeper gloves, Zico went off to Italy almost a year before, Cláudio Adão went to Botafogo and Cleo returned to Palmeiras.

Claudio García set up the axis of the team: Leandro, Figueiredo, Mozer, Júnior, Andrade, Adílio, Tita, Lico and Nunes. To make the club better, Argentine legend Fillol was brought in, the starting goalkeeper for the 1978 Argentina World Cup winners. Left-winger João Paulo arrived from Santos. In the first round of the 84th Brazilian Championship, 40 clubs were divided into eight groups with five clubs each. Three qualified for the second round from each group, 24 in total, but the third-placed team still had a knockout play-off, advancing another four.

Flamengo ended the first group with four wins and four draws. Behind them were Palmeiras. In the second round, Flamengo won three matches, lost two in Rio Grande do Sul, with a 4-0 loss to Internacional, and drew one, which was good for second place. It did get better for Flamengo, starting with three straight wins and two draws to win their group. They moved on to face Corinthians, where they won 2-0 with goals from Elder and Bebeto. Unfortunately, the club got eliminated by São Paulo 4-1. This caused Claudio García to quit as manager.

As the 1983 Brazilian champions, Flamengo were put into Group 3 of the Libertadores with Santos, América de Cali and Junior, as the winner was the only one to advance. Flamengo had a great group season: against Santos, they won 4-1, they drew 1-1 with América de Cali and they beat second-placed Junior 2-1. They finished the group with another big win, 5-0, over Santos, and then won the group at home against América de Cali 4-2. One of the reasons for the great play was the hiring of the new manager, the world-renowned Zagallo. Grêmio took Flamengo out of the Libertadores, where they fell in the final to Independiente from Argentina.

In the second half of the season, the club would undergo very few changes. Sadly, young defender Figueiredo died in a single-engine plane crash during the State Championship, travelling between Rio de Janeiro and Salvador. Three others left: Lico retired, Marinho was sold to Atlético Mineiro and Lúcio went to América. Jorginho, a young right-back, came in from América.

Flamengo had a great start to the Guanabara Cup, winning nine out of 11 matches in the first round. They drew against Goytacaz and lost to Vasco. The Taça Rio, on the other hand, was an absolute horror show for the club. They started out by losing to Volta Redonda, and drew with Olaria, Vasco, Bangu and Campo Grande. Finally, they were put out of their misery by losing to Fluminense.

To become the champions of Rio, the triangular final included Flamengo (Guanabara Cup winner), Vasco (Rio Cup winner) and Fluminense. It all came down to another Fla–Flu match to decide the title. For the second consecutive year, this time in front of 153,000 fans at the Maracanã, Assis sent the Flamengo supporters home sad, as he won it, 1-0, for Fluminense. This sent the club into another rethink about the players – mainly this time, it was the attack. Forwards Nunes and Edmar left the club, to be replaced by right-winger Heyder, Chiquinho and Marquinhos.

Going into the Brazilian Championship of 1985, the club had to face yet another change in format. In the first round, 44 clubs were divided into four groups, two with ten and two with 12 clubs. The teams from Group A only faced those in Group B, with Group C facing only those from Group D. The round winners in each group went to round two, with the top two placed in each group in addition to the winners. Therefore, going into the second round was four from each group. In the first round, Flamengo beat Santa Cruz, Corinthians, Palmeiras, Coritiba, América and Grêmio. They drew with Atlético Mineiro and Fluminense, while losing to Botafogo and Guarani. This put them through to the second round, where they beat Santa Cruz 7-0 and Botafogo 6-1. In the semi-finals, Flamengo had Bahia, Ceará and Brasil de Pelotas. Flamengo struggled, drawing with Ceará and Bahia, then beating Brasil de Pelotas at the Maracanã.

In the final stretch of the season, Flamengo and Rio de Janeiro got into bed with each other to make the club better. Zico came back from Udinese after two years, and Galinho de Quintino followed. However, with this good feeling, Flamengo were eliminated from the Brazilian national tournament, spurring on another crisis with the club. Out the door went manager Zagallo and his assistant Américo Faria, and in came Zico's brother, Edu Coimbra. However, despite the confusion and madness of the season, Joubert was the one who actually ended up taking over the team. Fillol transferred to Atlético Madrid, and Tita left for Internacional. Goalkeeper Zé Carlos came up from the junior team. The 1985 Carioca was tragic not only for Flamengo, but for the rest of football. In the second round against Bangu at the Maracanã, one of Bangu's right-backs went studs up into Zico's legs, breaking one of them and causing significant damage to his knee. This would affect Zico for the rest of his life, and drive him to play in Asia.

Zico's injury devastated the club, as they drew with Bangu, Americano, América and Fluminense. They lost to Portuguesa and lost in the last round to Vasco. Out the door was Joubert as manager, and next up was his assistant coach Sebastião Lazaroni. In the Rio Cup, the play got better as they only lost points with draws with Bangu, América and Fluminense. Flamengo needed an extra match to proceed in the tournament after tying with Bangu on eight wins and three draws. They beat Bangu 1-0 with a goal by Adílio, putting them in the triangular finals. Sadly, another loss to Fluminense and a 2-1 defeat to Bangu knocked out Flamengo. Fluminense ended up beating Bangu to become three-time champions of Rio de Janeiro.

It was hoped that 1986 could be a building year for the club, but right after the end of the Carioca of 1985 was the Carioca of 1986. To make up for the lack of Zico in the middle, the club brought in Sócrates from Fiorentina. Sadly, the thought of Andrade, Adílio, Sócrates and Zico being the greatest midfield in Brazil wasn't to be, as Sócrates and Zico's legs wouldn't allow it.

Zico returned after a year in the 4-1 rout of Fluminense with a hat-trick from Zico, and one from Bebeto. Finally, the great rivals had been vanquished, and this got the supporters thinking only good things for the season. What made them even happier was they saw a very good defensive core with Jorginho, Leandro, Mozer and Adalberto. They also had a very young Bebeto playing up front. Sadly, again, knee problems and absences would affect it. Sócrates never played in the Carioca, Zico only three times, Mozer twice and Leandro once before a knee injury took him out.

The fans' enthusiasm was at fever pitch as the club beat Portuguesa 4-0 in the second round. In the first eight rounds, there was only one draw, against Americano – the rest were wins. In the final stretch, a defeat by Bangu and a draw with Goytacaz allowed rivals Vasco to get closer in the standings of the Guanabara Cup. To decide the round, Vasco and Flamengo met, but the red and blacks were turned away by two goals by future Flamengo player Romário.

In the Rio Cup, the first round was a forgettable performance as they drew with Campo Grande and lost to Botafogo. They further lost points in draws against Americano and Bangu, but took the lead in the group with another win over Fluminense, 1-0. In the second round, all Flamengo needed was to beat Vasco to reach the final. In the first half, two great attackers of the generation put on displays, as Bebeto scored for Flamengo and Romário scored one for Vasco. The match would not stop there. Roberto Dinamite put Vasco ahead right after the break. Flamengo struck back with goals from Bebeto on 36 minutes and Júlio César Barbosa on 39, making the final score 3-2. It was enough to send them to the Carioca Final, against the same club, Vasco. The first two legs of the final ended in goalless draws, forcing a third game. The final match was at the Maracanã, and it saw Bebeto and Júlio César Barbosa score the deciding goals for the title. This was the first piece of silverware for the club since the golden era.

During the second half of the season, the main change was at number 9 after Chiquinho was sold to Benfica. In his place was Kita, and a left-back named Airton was brought in. The Brazilian Championship went through another change yet again: 44 clubs were divided into four groups of 11, and the top six moved to the second phase, with 12 more with the best campaigns. Zico was out for the entire tournament, and during the last part, left-back Adalberto, a young player from the academy, fractured his leg against Botafogo. The club did well, winning five and losing two only, to Corinthians and Atlético Paranaense. Flamengo won the group, advancing with Ponte Preta, Corinthians, Atlético Paranaense and América.

In the second round, the remaining 36 clubs were divided into four groups of nine, with the top four advancing to the knockout round. The good news was that Sócrates had recovered enough to help them win six, although they did lose five. They finished third in their group behind Guarani and Fluminense. They were ahead of Grêmio, and had to face Atlético Mineiro. Traditional powers Internacional, Santos and Botafogo failed to qualify for the round of 16.

This year was highlighted by bringing silverware back to the club.

Off the back of this bad campaign, the club brought in Renato Gaúcho from Grêmio and Sidney from São Paulo in the 1986 Brazilian Championship. Zico only played five of the 31 matches in the 1987 Carioca Championship. The season did not start well for the club, as they lost 2-0 in the second round of the Guanabara Cup to Porto Alegre. Next, they lost to Americano, but these were the only two losses the club had in the Guanabara Cup. The campaign was full of matches ending 0-0 with such clubs as Mesquita, Botafogo, Fluminense, América and Vasco. Because of the bad start, the club fired manager Sebastião Lazaroni, and elevated his assistant Carlinhos, for his second stint as caretaker boss, for the time being.

For the Rio Cup the manager was Antônio Lopes, who had been at Vasco da Gama when the club were the Rio champions in 1982 over Flamengo. The Rio Cup was on script for the year: the club only lost once in the second round to Bangu, and drew a lot of matches: Cabofriense, Vasco, Campo Grande and Fluminense.

The last round was in front of 5,000 fans at the Caio Martins Stadium in Niterói and it was Zico's first match in the Carioca of 1987. With the legend back in the side, the difficult situation in the season was reversed for a match, a 1-0 win over Fluminense through Marquinhos to get through the round. The club reached the final, and Zico being around got the supporters dreaming of the title.

The triangular final for the Carioca Championships was between Vasco (Guanabara Cup winners), Bangu (Rio Cup champions) and Flamengo (third-round champions). Vasco and Flamengo beat Bangu, meaning the title would be decided in the final game; 114,000[33] spectators at the Maracanã were there to see Vasco versus Flamengo for the title. Added spice to the match was that former Flamengo manager Sebastião Lazaroni had turned up at Vasco as the manager. Also Tita was in the side for Vasco, and he would steal the title for them to hurt his former team, with a goal in the first half.

In the second half of the season, Mozer, Adílio, Marquinhos and Sidney all left. Two veterans were brought in to strengthen the squad – defender Edinho, and Nunes returned. A young Bebeto would also be part of the set-up as well. This was all a lead-up to the most troubled Brazilian Championship to date. In the 1987 edition, the traditional club rebelled against the CBF because the last model was unprofitable, and the level of competitiveness only increased after the third round. The CBF was not completely at fault; there was a serious economic crisis engulfing the country. As already mentioned in the book, the strongest associations of the sport in Brazil got together, forming the Clube dos 13; these were Flamengo, Vasco, Fluminense, Botafogo, Corinthians, Palmeiras, São Paulo, Santos, Grêmio, Internacional, Cruzeiro, Atlético Mineiro and Bahia. The group invited three other clubs, Santa Cruz, Coritiba and Goiás, to form a tournament called Copa União. The tournament included only 16 clubs facing each other in a single round. The first four would advance to a semi-final and a final knockout.

These 16 teams would play in the green group, while another 16 were placed in the yellow group – Guarani, Portuguesa de Desportos, Inter de Limeira, Bangu,

---

33 http://livroanacao.blogspot.com/

América-RJ, Atlético Paranaense, Vitória, Sport Recife, Náutico, Criciúma, Atlético Goianiense, Ceará, Joinville, CSA, Treze and Rio Branco. The blue and white groups were also formed with 24 clubs. Clubs were picked on economic criteria, and that provoked protests among the excluded group, like Guarani, the Brazilian vice-champion of 1986, América do Rio, the third-placed team in the Brazilian Championship, and Bangu, the Brazilian vice-champion of 1985.

Flamengo kicked off the tournament by losing to São Paulo with goals from Müller and Careca at the Maracanã. This caused Antõnio Lopes, the Flamengo manager, to resign, though most thought he was fired. This had never happened – firing a coach in the first round – and it showed the beginning of emotional decisions in club management. Emotions overrode rational choices, which showed a total lack of understanding in the planning of the football department. It was almost like 'charity managers', a term coined by American soccer podcaster Simon Allen, was the name of the game. Just get someone to do a poor job.

In the second round, Carlinhos took over as interim again, but then got the job full-time later on. With Carlinhos in charge, Flamengo beat Vasco 2-1 with goals from Bebeto and Zico. Sadly, this good luck did not last, as there was a goalless draw with Santos, and two straight losses to Internacional and Fluminense. The club did get back on track briefly with a win over Coritiba, but there were also draws against Goiás and Cruzeiro. It was a modest campaign for the club, with two wins, three draws and three defeats. They qualified for a short tournament which only had 15 rounds and no return. Flamengo seemed like they would be short of the strength to fight, ranking among the top four to advance. Such was the case in a loss to Botafogo, a draw with Grêmio and another loss to Atlético Mineiro.

Flamengo had other plans, and with four rounds remaining, the club took off. There was a 2-0 win over Palmeiras at the Maracanã, a 2-0 away victory over Bahia, a draw against Corinthians at Pacaembu and a 3-1 victory over Santa Cruz back at the Maracanã, where Zico scored all the goals. The club finished first, advancing to the semifinal against Atlético Mineiro.

In the first match of the two-legged final at the Maracanã, Bebeto scored the only goal in the match. In the return match at Mineirão, Flamengo started off rolling on 31 minutes in the first half, up 2-0 with goals from Bebeto and Zico, but Atlético had a very strong team. They came storming back in the second half, equalising with a goal by Sérgio Araújo. On 34 minutes in the second half, however, Zico stole the ball and passed it to Renato Gaúcho, who dribbled it into the empty goal for a 3-2 win and a final against Internacional.

This would be the first match to settle the tie between the two clubs with three titles in each format in the championship since 1971. The first match was at Estádio Beira-Rio, in Porto Alegre, and it ended in a 1-1 draw. Bebeto scored for Flamengo – Amarildo for Inter. The return match on a rainy Sunday afternoon was at the Maracanã. All that was needed was a long pass by Andrade to Bebeto at the beginning of the match. Bebeto, with his great touch, put the ball past goalkeeper Taffarel. Flamengo held on for the title win. The club were finally national champions again, and the mood was very good going into the 1988 season.

They did lose some players after the title, which is common. Airton went to Grêmio, Kita went to Portuguesa de Desportos and Nunes left again for Volta Redonda. The only player coming in was young midfielder Luis Henrique from Bahia. He only played 26 matches for the club but carved a massive career for himself, eventually ending up in Europe at Monaco.

The club kept winning, collecting the Guanabara Cup after winning eight of the first ten matches and drawing against Botafogo and Bangu. The cup was won with a victory over América. Then the form came crashing down, after being guaranteed a place in the final of the State Championship. In the Rio Cup, while winning five of the first seven matches, they lost to América and Volta Redonda. They did lose in the first round to Fluminense. In the following three rounds, they lost to Vasco and drew with Botafogo and Fluminense. Zico was barely on the field, playing only six matches in the State Championship. The fans' spirit took a nosedive after this.

The third round was a quadrangular format, and the club drew with Fluminense and beat Americano. They lost to Vasco yet again 3-1. In the final, Flamengo got Vasco again. Each team started out with one bonus point, and whoever got four points were declared champions. Vasco won the first match 2-1, even with Bebeto opening the scoring early, but Bismarck and Romário won it, leading Vasco to three points. One more draw would confirm the title for Vasco. The match dragged on with a goalless scoreline, until Cocada scored the goal to beat Flamengo for the fourth time, and win the title for Vasco.

The board was frustrated by not being able to defend the title, so they overhauled the squad for the second part of the season. For the most part, they were forced into this after getting a big transfer offer from Roma in Italy for Renato

Gaúcho and Andrade. Midfielder Júlio César Barbosa was sold to Racing Santander. Coming in were Uruguayan defender Darío Pereyra, defensive midfielder Paulo Martins, Luvanor and Sérgio Araújo. From the youths were Valmir and Gérson. To complete the clean sweep, former Santos manager Candinho was brought in to steady the ship.

The Copa União brought together 24 clubs divided into two groups of 12. Again, the championship was changed, as a victory was worth three points and not two. In the first round, all tied matches went to a penalty shoot-out, the winner receiving two points for the standings. Also, in the first round it was made so that every club played against everyone. The top two of each group made it to the quarter-finals.

The season started off with another defeat to Vasco, a fifth in a row. Flamengo still beat América and Corinthians, but lost to Bahia and drew with Santa Cruz at the Maracanã, losing on penalties. This bad start was due to Zico only playing in the Vasco loss. He left the match due to pain in his knee, and did not return until the eighth round. Candinho departed as manager after the fifth round. Eventually, former Brazilian manager Telê Santana came in as head coach.

With Telê guiding the side and Zico's return, the club beat Guarani 5-1, won 3-0 over Criciúma at the Maracanã, and drew with Cruzeiro and Coritiba. They finished in fifth place behind Fluminense, Internacional, Portuguese Sports and Atlético Mineiro. In the second round, Flamengo defied the odds and played better. Starting out, they lost the first three out of five matches. They did beat Sport Recife though.

In the final round, the club took off, winning five of the last six matches: Fluminense, Atlético Paranaense,

Portuguesa de Desportos, Bangu and Atlético Mineiro, and only drawing against Goiás. Flamengo finished the round in second place behind Sport Recife, putting them through to the quarter-finals. They faced Grêmio, and the first match was a goalless draw at Estádio Olímpico in Porto Alegre. Again, however, Flamengo would end up losing, when Cuca scored the goal to eliminate them. Not the end that the board wanted, but they decided to keep Telê Santana. They did prune the squad a bit: Darío Pereyra, Luvanor, Paulo Martins, Declacir and Henágio all left. Striker Nando was the only incoming player.

That all sounds bleak, but coming from the academy was a generation of talent: defenders Aldair and Zé Carlos II, left-back Leonardo, defensive midfielder Flávio, midfielder Zé Ricardo and striker Alcindo. There were more to follow, with defenders Júnior Baiano, Rogério and Gonçalves, and midfielders Marquinhos, Luis Antônio, Luís Carlos, Marcelinho and Djalminha. All those players would end up being very good for the club. The Carioca in 1989 was entirely from around Rio in Gáea, with the selected presence of outsiders, Renato Carioca and Sérgio Araújo.

The Guanabara Cup of 1989 started with a typical stumbling block, a goalless draw with Porto Alegre. Following that, a 4-2 win over Bangu, two 4-0 wins over Fluminense and Cabofriense and an 8-1 win over newly promoted Nova Cidade. Bebeto and Renato Carioca were fighting goal for goal for top scorer in the championship. Finally, the club beat Vasco 3-1 in the last round to put them through to the final. In the Rio Cup, Porto Alegre provided Flamengo with a headache, beating them 3-1. Flamengo were up 3-1 against Botafogo, but lost the lead by giving up two goals. Again, the club missed out on the title, surprisingly to Botafogo. In the State Final, again the club came second, losing to Botafogo again.

After yet another failure, the board hired the big guns for a big season. Renato Gaúcho came back from Roma and Borghi came in. Vasco made heavy investments in players too for the 1988/89 season. Flamengo and Vasco's rivalry was very fierce in the market. The defence was a concern, as Aldair went to Benfica and Zé Carlos II to Porto. Furthermore, Gonçalves went to Botafogo and Jorginho went to Bayer Leverkusen. So the club had to bring in defender Fernando and ex-Vasco player Márcio Rossini from Bangu. In the spirit of making the club better, they did not stop there; in came goalkeeper Zé Carlos Paulista, right-back Josimar and Uidemar.

Before getting into the Brazilian Championship, Flamengo had to partake in a new competition, the Copa do Brasil. They made it to the semi-finals, after eliminating Paysandu, Blumenau and Corinthians. Grêmio were the opponents for the chance to play in the finals. In the first match, Flamengo got a 2-0 lead, only to have it erased by Grêmio for a draw in the end. In the second match, Grêmio throttled Flamengo 6-1 to make the final. At this point, Telê Santana's seat was getting very warm. The club kept him for the next three matches, but the form did not get any better. Telê went back to São Paulo after getting sacked, and started winning again, with the Brazilian Championship in 1991, the Copa Libertadores in 1992 and the Mundial in 1993.

The 1989 Brazilian National Tournament had 22 clubs, in two groups of 11. The first eight in each group moved on to the next round. Flamengo finished sixth behind Corinthians, Botafogo, Atlético Mineiro, Náutico and Inter de Limeira. They finished ahead of São Paulo and

Internacional. In the three matches after Telê was sacked, the caretaker was João Carlos, and he beat Botafogo and Guarani, while drawing with Vitória. The next manager was Valdir Espinosa, recommended by Renato Gaúcho, who had won the 1983 Intercontinental Cup and Copa Libertadores with Renato Gaúcho at Grêmio. With Espinosa in charge, it was a strange year. They beat Vasco 2-0 with two goals from under-20 forward Bujica, ending Vasco's unbeaten record. Espinosa presided over a 5-0 rout of Fluminense, which was Zico's last match. But Flamengo finished fifth behind São Paulo, Botafogo, Corinthians and Atlético Mineiro.

With Zico off, and the new decade starting in 1990, the club trimmed more players: Catarelli, Sergio Araúgio, Borghi, Nando, Márcio Rossini and Renato Carioca. In January of the same year, the under-20 team, managed by Ernesto Paulo, won their first Copa São Paulo de Juniores, the main national tournament at that level. Almost all of the players ended up playing in the first team eventually, and often. Flamengo beat Corinthians 7-1 with five goals from Djalminha. Players did arrive for the Campeonato Carioca, in André Cruz from Ponte Preta, Edu Marangon and Gaúcho from Palmeiras. With all this youth in the side, the team in the Guanabara Cup did not lose in the first nine matches, but drew four times, against Fluminense, América, Americano and Vasco. The last two matches were defeats to Bangu and Botafogo. Right-back was a bad spot for the club; Josimar was not playing, so Uidemar and young Mário Carlos ended up platooning in the Rio Cup. And the club fumbled its chance at the Carioca Final, as they started out drawing with Itaperuna and Cabofriense, not exactly top sides. Flamengo ended up losing to Fluminense and Vasco, which cost them the title. To add insult to injury, they also lost to Botafogo, which meant Valdir Espinosa was fired.

The glory time was also a World Cup year, and in Brazil it is a big deal. This was a side that was supposed to win it all. The talent all over the field was remarkable, the managing great also. Stuart Horsfield wrote a book about it: *1982 Brazil: The Glorious Failure*. These were supposed to be the best of the era, like the Mighty Magyars of 1954 and Johan Cruyff's 1974 team. They also became one of the best to never win the cup.

Like with anything to do with the Brazilian national team, there was the pomp and circumstance of a grandiose party. The 1982 Brazil lined up for the finals to a soundtrack of samba drums and dancing, ascending down the stands of Estadio Ramón Sánchez Pizjuán, a show that any stadium would expect. With the growth of specialised media, many people had become tactical experts, and they wondered how manager Telê Santana set up his tactics. The most common thought was a 4-2-2-2 formation, pushing full-backs wide, with two holding midfielders providing a double pivot for the attacking midfielders who provided service for the front two. Sometimes, it would turn into a chaotic and cavalier commitment to attacking football, appearing to be a 2-7-1. This unique formation had two centre-halves staying back, full-backs providing width to the midfield and just a lone striker.

Going into the games, Toninho Cerezo was on the last match of his three-game ban, after being sent off in a qualifier against Bolivia. So Santana had to bring in Roberto Falcão to replace him. Falcão was a legend in Rome, being nicknamed the 'Eighth King of Rome' by the Roma fans. He didn't join the squad until May after the Serie A season had finished. Falcão, a deep-lying playmaker, was the Brazilian footballer of the year in 1978 and 1979, and going to Europe had limited his time with Brazil. In fact, he didn't play for the national side between 1979 and 1982.

Because of this, he was one of the last players named in the squad, playing in the final two warm-up games. Santana, in these two games, saw Falcão's organisational ability, leadership and experience in the European game. Cerezo was no slouch either – he was a deep-lying playmaker with a beautiful range of passing. Santana was familiar with him, having coached him during their stay at Atlético Mineiro. With them was Éder, who had exceptional physical strength and power. He wasn't fast and didn't have a want to work hard for the team, but he could bend a ball with the outside of his left foot like no other.

We all know how great a player Zico was, being the classic number 10. He was the South American player of the year in 1981 and 1982, and regarded as the second-greatest Brazilian player of all time behind Pelé. Technically, he was perfect: he could link the play between the midfield and the strikers, pass with both feet and had great vision. For as great as he was, there was the enigmatic Sócrates. He was a deep thinker, an intelligent man, a trained doctor, and that was his good side. Sócrates was a different athlete; he smoked and drank to excess. Ability-wise, he could play anywhere on the pitch with poise and balance. His grace and skill made the game look so simple. By 1982 he had an almost telepathic understanding with his international team-mates.

Sócrates had very long legs, and never wore shin pads. He made his career by dictating the pace and style of the side without much physical exertion. For the 1982 World Cup, he gave up smoking to change his body for good.

Against the USA in Seville, Brazil had a stuttering start, which may have been because of their inexperience at major tournaments. Sócrates, ever the showman, with 15 minutes left, let off a thunderous strike to ignite Brazil's World Cup campaign. This whipped the fans into a frenzy, as they tried to get another piece of artistry out of the side. With two minutes left, Isidoro put a ball into Falcão, who allowed it to run through his legs as if it was planned. Éder appeared from nowhere and, as he was running, flicked the ball with his left foot and hit a powerful volley with the same foot, which won the game 2-1. The next match was the same, a slow start for Brazil and then breathtakingly beautiful play to win 4-1.

New Zealand, an international pushover were dispatched the same way. The passing was a joy to watch; it wasn't like the tiki-taka that Barcelona played and was copied by everyone. This was ten- to 20-yard one- and two-touch passes, with every part of the foot used to move the ball. Next up, Argentina and a young Diego Maradona.

Even with Maradona, Argentina were no match for Brazil. Éder's 35-yard kick bounced off the crossbar into the path of Zico, who put it in the back of the net for 1-0. Next up, a right-sided cross from Falcão to Serginho for a far-post header. Then, to really show off their beauty, Zico took a ball 30 yards out, went through four players, threaded a ball to Flamengo team-mate Júnior, who tucked the ball under Argentine goalkeeping legend Ubaldo Fillol for the third goal.

This set up the final group game against Italy. The Italians had only beaten Argentina 2-1, so why would Brazil have to worry about them? Clearly, Brazil were better. They had all the talent and could win out of a seeming defeat.

Zico in the second Toyota Cup, Flamengo 3-0 Liverpool in Tokyo on 12 December 1981

Zico and Kenny Dalglish in the second Toyota Cup, Flamengo 3-0 Liverpool

23 November 2019, Éverton Ribeiro during the 2019 Copa Libertadores Final

The Maracanã – Flamengo's home stadium

Previous page: Flamengo fans turn out to welcome new signing Ronaldinho

Club World Cup Final, Liverpool FC v Flamengo, Jorge Jesus

Romário celebrates his fourth goal, 7 October 1999

A Flamengo supporter before the start of the Brazilian Championship Final match against Grêmio

The Liverpool FC tour bus parade in their honour after winning the 1981 European Cup Final against Real Madrid 1-0

Medal of champions of the 2019 Copa Libertadores Final between Flamengo and River Plate

An aerial view of Christ the Redeemer in Rio de Janeiro

Rafinha celebrates the victory after the 2019 Copa Libertadores Final between Flamengo and River Plate

What followed was one of the greatest World Cup matches of all times. Italy took the lead from a wide-open Paolo Rossi, who was playing during his ban, for a 1-0 start.

Sócrates and Zico played it back and forth, going around Claudio Gentile, before Zico put the ball past Dino Zoff for their goal. But the Italians were never out of it, as a lapse of judgement from Cerezo gave Rossi his second goal. The second half was a contrast in the different styles the nations were known for. One was the continuous waves of Brazilian attacks, and the other was the Italians' mastery of defending a one-goal lead while making counter-attacks.

Eventually, Brazil's constant attacks took their toll as Sócrates rolled the ball to Falcão. Cerezo, trying to make up for his mistake, ran around the back of him to create an overlapping full-back. With that move he took out Antonio Cabrini, Marco Tardelli, Gaetano Scirea and everyone else in the stadium, and Falcão put the ball back in the net for 2-2. Brazil were a point away from the semi-finals. As we know, they didn't go through.

There are many articles and media coverage that have been published about why the nation went out. However, they did have some good points during the tournament – in their five games, they scored 15 goals. Seven different outfield players scored. It was their philosophy, imagination, style and grace that made this a memorable tournament. However, this group never played together again. That's part of the magic lying behind all of this.

So after this disappointment, Brazil had to regroup. A favoured nation like this couldn't take the disappointment and stay the same. The hierarchy of Brazilian soccer had to dump Telê Santana and his style of playing the game.

In place of the beautiful football had to be a brutalist, physical football. The man they turned to was Kuwait's manager during the 1982 World Cup in Spain, Carlos Alberto Parreira. He was a physical trainer and part of Mario Zagallo's staff at the 1970 World Cup. Parreira was a strong proponent, like his mentor Zagallo, of physical and defensive training.

He was put in charge of preparing for the 1986 World Cup. In the back of his mind, he did realise he could be out of a job very quickly. Parreira described the national team as a laboratory, because he had to change so much. By 1986, Zico, Sócrates and Júnior would all be 33 or older. As much as Sócrates took care of himself for the 1982 World Cup, his bad habits could pick back up again. Slowly, Parreira kept moving the 1982 squad out the door, but he kept most of the home-based stars, plus Falcão and Edinho.

They played their first friendly under Parreira on 28 April 1983 against Chile. It was an unimpressive 3-2 and it was obvious that Brazil were weak in goal. So Parreira called in Émerson Leão and Acácio for their European tour. He was also able to bring in Tita, defenders Marinho and Márcio Rossini, and striker João Paulo. Flamengo's defensive pair Leandro and Júnior were in the midst of a loss of form but were still recalled.

Santana, for all the international love, played without much of a thought about defensive organisation. Good technique wasn't enough; fouls in dangerous situations and physical strength were key for the game in the 1980s. Parreira's training sessions involved defensive aspects of the game, and defending corners. The said tour was scheduled for June, and Brazil were to play Portugal on the 8th, Wales on the 12th, Switzerland on the 17th and Sweden on the last day on 22 June. The 12 June game was supposed to have been West Germany, but they were unavailable.

After Parreira named his squad for the tour, he faced a problem he would rant about later in life: clubs refusing to release players for the national team. Flamengo withdrew their players because they had the Copa Libertadores and Brazilian Cup. That took out Zico, Leandro, Júnior and Marinho.

Zico was in the midst of being transferred to Udinese in Italy's Serie A. At the age of 30, he had to be sold because there was a law in Brazil that said that a player became a free agent after the age of 32. You did not want to lose Zico for nothing, so they were forced to sell him for a profit. Italian clubs, after seeing how the Brazilian 1982 team played, started approaching other players too. AC Milan and Roma approached Sócrates, but were denied. Éder was looked at by Ajman of the United Arab Emirates. Cerezo joined Roma that summer to play with Falcão.

Other players were withdrawn too: Paulo Roberto, Tita, Oscar, Renato, Nene, Dema and Reinaldo. To replace them, Parreira brought in Betão, Edson, Luizinho, Toninho Carlos and Alemão. Sócrates did go on the tour, so it would be a good one. It kicked off on 8 June versus Portugal in Coimbra, and the Brazilians played before 13,000, the lowest attendance they had appeared in front of. Brazil dominated the home team, winning 4-0 with goals from Sócrates, Pedrinho and a brace from Careca.

Next, Brazil moved on to Cardiff to play Wales on 12 June. Wales didn't generally play national teams with such status or talent. The 1982 team could have passed the Welsh team off the park. However, on this day the Welsh scored in the first five minutes. David Giles crossed from the left side and Brian Flynn scored a diving header. Paulo Isidoro tied it up for the away side.

It was then off to Basel to play Switzerland on 17 June, where again, as the theme always went, the opposition scored first.

In the 33rd minute, the Swiss scored from a penalty kick from André Egli. The spot kick was awarded after Márcio had fouled Braschler. Not to be outdone, in the second half Sócrates was pushed in the back in the box, and was awarded a penalty kick. Being the star and the deep thinker he was, he took the penalty himself and scored. With just a few minutes left in the game, Careca scored the winning goal from close range.

The last match of the tour had a sentimental aspect to it. It was against Sweden, a country that in 1958 were their opponents when Brazil won their first World Cup. The score in that game was 5-2, so there was something akin in this game. This was the most entertaining match of the tour. Brazil opened up the scoring in the seventh minute, as Márcio back-heeled a corner in. Sweden then put two in the back of the net in quick succession.

Sure enough, Brazil came back to level the score. Thomas Ravelli swung a ball in from the left which missed, but Careca headed in the rebound. The back and forth nature of the game meant that Sweden had to get in on it, and in the 33rd minute Corneliusson put in the third goal. Late in the second half, Sócrates sent in a pass to Jorginho for the leveller.

In the 76th minute, Sócrates sent in a through ball from the middle for Jorginho, who dribbled past Ravelli and scored the equalising goal. The tour wasn't a success, as the defensive play on the field wasn't fun to watch. Sócrates was being watched by Serie A teams, and eventually moved to Fiorentina.

In 1983 back in Rio, Flamengo would have some great times. They played a match at the Maracanã in front of the largest paying audience ever registered in a Brazilian Championship match. It was 155,523[34] in a second-leg match against Santos on 29 May. Zico got the party going early, getting a goal in the first minute, followed by Leandro and Adílio. In the first leg in Morumbi, Santos had won 2-1. Flamengo played with Raul, Leandro, Figueiredo, Marinho, Júnior, Vitor, Adílio, Éder, Zico; Baltazar (Robertinho) and Júlio César (Ademir).

The players from the great team stayed in the squad. An important reinforcement was striker Baltazar, who ended the Brazilian Championship as the team's top scorer in the competition with 13. Zico was still at his best with 17 goals. Brazilian legendary defender Carlos Alberto Torres was the manager for the title.

Ironically, Sócrates came back to Brazil in 1985, leaving the year before for Italy because of the military junta. Sócrates arrived back with a good friend of his, Zico. They both transferred to Flamengo together. The problem was, by this time, Sócrates's legs were betraying him and they were only on the pitch together for 20 matches. One of the times they got on the pitch together was during the Fla–Flu on 16 February 1986, and despite Fluminense being in a golden era, it was still a derby. Flamengo dominated the proceedings, with Zico scoring a hat-trick.

During that match, the line-up was Cantarele, Jorginho, Leandro, Mozer, Adalberto, Andrade, Sócrates, Zico,

---

34 www.flamengo.com.br/historia

Bebeto, Chiquinho and Adílio. This was a great line-up that would, in theory, be the one contesting the 1986 Carioca Championship, trying to regain the title. The previous attempts had come up short in each of the last four years. Ironically, this was the line-up used for the 4-1 win over the three-time champions Fluminense.

Zico is the greatest scorer in the history of Fla–Flu with 19 goals, one more than Flamengo's Pirillo, and five more than Fluminense's Hércules. Zico, before he left for Italy, already had 14 goals against the great rivals, and commanded great routs in 1976, 4-1, 1978, 4-0, and 1982, 3-0. This was a different Zico, however, as his knees were beginning to go out on him. On 29 August 1985, he also suffered that knee injury at the hands of Márcio Nunes that started the downfall of his career. The injury forced him to have surgery and he missed four months, making his return a question mark. How would he come back? When he entered the field on 16 February, he put aside all the doubts with another great performance.

In the first ten minutes, Zico started a great play, where he passed the ball to Bebeto; then while running with Adílio, he played a two-man touch back and forth, going around his mark and hitting Bebeto again. Adílio got a hold of it and crossed to Zico for a diving header for 1-0. Leomir for Fluminense in the 43rd minute converted a penalty for the opposition, but that would be the last goal for them.

Into the second half, and on six minutes in, after a good display of passing, Zico scored his second, to keep his debut one for the ages. The play got more frenetic as both sides tried to get this game done with. On 32 minutes, Zico converted a penalty kick just after Bebeto had got in on the scoring, putting one past Cantarele, and the match ended

4-1. This was the first match of the season in the Carioca, and the final match for Flamengo, after many delays, was against Vasco on 10 August 1986.

In the summer of 1986, the World Cup was in Mexico, and Flamengo lost three very good players in Mozer, Zico and Sócrates. The favourites for the title were the Fla–Flu teams and Vasco, all big teams in Rio. There was a lot of talent among the Rio teams: Romário was just starting his career at Vasco, and Fluminense had Vitor and Paulo Roberto. Flamengo, while not having great players, had some very talented ones still around: Guto, Zé Carlos II, Waltinho, Júlio César Barbosa, Chiquinho and the very talented Bebeto. Without the three great players, Flamengo had to motor on, like in their match against Botafogo, as Chiquinho and Bebeto scored the goals early on.

Bebeto was quickly coming good. He pulled off a shot that was similar to the 1970 goal Pelé scored against Uruguay's Mazurkiewicz, this time against Luiz Carlos at the Maracanã. In the next match against Mesquita in the fourth round, Adílio suffered a sprained left knee and missed significant time after that. He was replaced by academy player Zinho, who became another great player to come out of Rio. Also in the match, another player was promoted from the academy in defender Aldair. Slowly, the youth was being integrated into the first team. The high rate of academy players coming into the squad was because of new manager Sebastião, who took over the first team in October 1985 during the Carioca Championship.

The start of the Rio Cup was strange, with a draw against Campo Gande (1-1), a victory over América at the Maracanã (2-0) and a defeat against Botafogo (2-1). Then the club took off with a 5-0 win over Portuguesa da Ilha.

What made this odd was that Leandro made this his last match. Then, Zico would play three more matches before suffering another injury. Mozer was cut from the World Cup for knee surgery after only two games. Sócrates and Cantarele were now no longer part of the club. The title would have to come from the talented youth from the academy.

There was a great crop coming through: Zé Carlos was very good in goal, Guto and Aidair were top defenders, Aílton was the workman in the midfield along with Waltinho, Vinícius was a very confident number 9, Zinho was a very good left-winger, Alcindo was well known on the right, and Bebeto, Jorginho and Adalberto were great in their positions. Now, with the youth in the side, Flamengo were off to the races for the title. They won against Goytacaz and Mesquita, drew with Americano, won against Olaria and Fluminense, and drew 1-1 with Bangu.

Coming to the end, Fluminense were in the lead for the Rio Cup with a 1-0 win over Bangu, which meant that the deciding match was against Flamengo if Fluminense wanted to win the title again. Flamengo had to get through Vasco first, and they had most of their talented legends with them. Flamengo won 3-2 to lift the Rio Cup and win the State Final.

Chapter 10

The 90s

JUST BEING Flamengo meant that they could get great players to come to Rio. Zico suffered a horrible knee injury and had to step away from the club for the last time during his playing days. The 90s were flashy but fun, and sometimes very painful. Money started pouring into the game around the world, and the Bosman ruling in Europe helped take away the death hold clubs had on their players. This made it possible for players to fail in Europe and come to South America without any repercussions.

One of the great players after Zico left was Renato Gaúcho. And while he never reached the heights of Zico, he was still very well thought of. Renato was a great scorer, who was very tough, had perfect positioning, was great in the air and had a fighting spirit. He was discovered by Gilson Aguiar, a scout at the club, and was brought in in May 1982. Renato was a defender when he first came in, but was moved up front to play right-wing and centre-forward. While in the academy, he formed an attacking line with Bebeto, Gilmar and Vinícius. Gaúcho was so good that he was nicknamed the 'new Zico'. On 6 June 1982 he made his professional debut, replacing Lico in a 2-0 victory over Desportiva in a friendly in Cariacica. It would be another two years before he would be in the top team again. In October 1984 he came on for Edmar in a 1-1 draw with Olaria at the Rua Bariri for the Taça Rio. The squad of 1985 didn't have any room for him, so he became a journeyman. He played for several Brazilian clubs, and even in Japan for Yomiuri. Eventually, he came back on loan from Palmeiras in January 1990, and was given the number 9 shirt. In his debut on 11 February against Cabofriense, Gaúcho scored the second goal in a 3-1 win. He scored 14 goals in the State Tournament – champions Botafogo's top scorers, Donizete and Paulo Roberto, had five each.

Flamengo returned to Tokyo to play in the Sharp Cup on 6 August 1990 and beat Real Sociedad 7-0. Gaúcho scored three, Renato, not the same guy, scored two, and Bujica and Bobô helped the cause by scoring one each to complete the rout. On the 12th, the team was off to win the Marlboro Cup on the synthetic flooring of the Giants Stadium, New Jersey, to beat Alianza Lima 1-0 with a Gaúcho goal. He would then, as a Flamengo starter, contribute five goals in the campaign for the first Copa do Brasil title in club history. In the season, Gaúcho scored 38 times.

Gaúcho became a permanent Flamengo player in 1991, but his team-mate Renato left for Botafogo. Gaúcho would be the man leading the line of a side with many talented young kids, loosely nicknamed 'Gaúcho's Boys'. Gaúcho's performance in the Libertadores was great; he scored eight times, once against Corinthians at Pacaembu (2-0), two against Nacional at the Maracanã (4-0), three against Deportivo Táchira in Venezuela (3-2) and two against Boca Juniors in the two-legged quarter-finals. Flamengo did not win the title, as they were eliminated by Boca Juniors at La Bombonera.

His great play would continue while playing in the Copa Rio, scoring one of the great goals against Americano in a 3-0 win. Gaúcho was under the management of Carlinhos, who put him with Paulo Nunes. They were fed with great service from Júnior, Marcelinho, Marquinhos, Djalminha and Nélio. Full-backs Charles Warrior and Piá whipped in great crosses. Gaúcho scored the winning goal in the 2-1 win in the Guanabara Cup against Botafogo. He was also prone to speaking his mind no matter who was around, including the referees. Time and time again he would score a goal when the club needed it most, like the winning one over Botafogo, 1-0, in the extra game that decided the Taça Rio. In the tournament, he would also be the top scorer again with 17 goals. And in 1991 he finished as the top scorer in the Copa Libertadores, the Super Cup and the State Championship. In the season, he was Flamengo's top scorer with 35.

He didn't stop his exceptional form in early 1992. In the first five rounds of the Brazilian Championship, he scored four times, and twice against São Paulo, a team that won the Libertadores. After this blazing start, he suffered a left thigh strain and missed two months. Once he came back, he was ever present in Flamengo's line-up, scoring two goals in the 3-1 win against Santos, and he was part of the build-up for the third goal.

On the field, Flamengo destroyed Botafogo with goals from Júnior, Nélio and Gaúcho, and a great goal by Piá, in just under 40 minutes. The next match against Botafogo was 2-0, after a dubious penalty won by Fabinho scored by Valdeir and a goal by Gaúcho. Gaúcho's greatest achievement at Flamengo was his last effort in the jersey. In the Campeonato Carioca 1992, while the Maracanã was under repairs, he was scoring at will.

Eventually, like all the greats at the time, he left for Serie A and a small club, Lecce. The Italian club had recently been promoted to Serie A, but Gaúcho did very little there. He returned to Brazil shortly after and played for several clubs, including Fluminense, until he hung up his boots in 1996 at 32 years old.

It was January 1990, and Flamengo were just into their first year after Zico had left for Japan. The club was at a crossroads. They had great players like Júnior, Leandro, at the end of his career, Renato Gaúcho, who we will mention more later on, Zinho and Leonardo. They did bring in other players like former Brazilian national-team player Edu Marangon from Torino, one who was thought of very highly at Portuguesa, to play the number 10 role. The youth set-up turned out some good players under the direction of Ernesto Paulo; they won the Rio de Janeiro championship and the Fernando Horta tournament. Now, Flamengo wanted the Copa São Paulo, which was partly a youth title.

During the first round of play, it was two points for a win, but if a team won with three or more points, it was three points. A tie was normal, at only one point and, unless it was 0-0, there would be a penalty shoot-out. Flamengo were in Group C in Santos with Criciúma, São Paulo, Botafogo de Ribeirão Preto, Nacional, Central Brasileira de Cotia and Santos. The first match was on Saturday, 6 January in Vila Belmiro against Botafogo-SP.

Flamengo put out a line-up of Adriano, Mário Carlos, Tita, Júnior Baiano, Piá (Sele), Fabinho, Marquinhos, Marcelinho, Djalminha, Paulo Nunes and Nélio. After just 15 minutes Flamengo were down, when Lúcio put the opposition ahead. Flamengo equalised on 36 minutes, with Fabinho scoring a goal after a cross from the left of the box.

But the result of the match wasn't only the draw – the first two absences occurred with the red cards of Júnior Baiano and Djalminha. For the match against Nacional two days later, they were replaced by Edmílson and Luiz Antônio. Flamengo eked out a win 1-0, with a goal from Hélio, but again had to deal with two more red-card expulsions in Marquinhos and coach Ernesto Paulo.

Following the match, Flamengo had to face surprise package Central Brasileira on the 10th, who had defeated Santos previously. Paulo Nunes made sure the same thing didn't happen to Flamengo, scoring a brace for the red and blacks. Nunes was then called up for the Brazilian youth team for the Copa Atlantica in Las Palmas, Spain, with Marquinhos and Marcelinho. It is always great for the club to get the young players competing in international matches in Europe. If Flamengo qualified for the next round, the players would go from those matches to the national team a couple of days later.

Flamengo travelled to Vila Belmiro on the 12th to face Circiúma and, with a returning Djalminha from suspension, opened the scoring in the first 12 minutes. However, Júnior Baiano had a shocker four minutes before half-time, allowing Everaldo to score. In the second half, Paulo Nunes scored again to secure the win for Flamengo. With a place in the next round secured, Flamengo just needed to face the hosts, Santos. The home fans weren't happy that their side had not yet qualified through to the next round. Santos supporters pelted the Flamengo team with stones, which stopped the match for 13 minutes while the mess was getting cleared up. Nélio and Mário Carlos retaliated for the Flamengo side and ended up being expelled. It wasn't a one-sided problem – César and França from Santos were thrown out too. When the game got going again, it finished 0-0 in regular time, so it went to penalties, with Flamengo winning 5-4.

In the first knockout phase, they were matched up against Tuna Luso from Pará, and this was played at Canindé on 16 January. It was an easy victory, 3-1, with goals by Piá, Marcelinho and Djalminha. That was followed up by a very talented Portuguesa, who had the best attack in the group, and the best campaign. They were led by Dener, and the attack would show their strength in the first half on 34 minutes, when Sinval put Portuguesa ahead. Marcelinho, the hero just before the end of the match, equalised for Flamengo. Off to a penalty shoot-out again, and Adriano became the saviour for Flamengo, saving all three shots by Portuguesa to seal the win. A sad aside to the match was that on 18 April 1994 in Rio de Janeiro, Dener lost his life in a car accident at the tender age of 23 when his car crashed into a tree on Borges de Medeiros Avenue.

The next phase would be different: the six clubs would be divided triangularly, called the green and yellow groups, with the first two being placed in the semi-finals. Flamengo were placed in the yellow group with Corinthians and Juventus da Mooca. The first match against Juventus, who were known for their youth production line, was at their stadium in Rua Javari, and it was a heavy field. Flamengo started off well, opening the scoring through Nélio after only eight minutes. Just before half-time, Piá knocked down Anderson in the area, and the referee signalled a penalty for Juventus. Adriano again was the rock between the pipes and turned away a strong, low kick from Ricardo. A minute later, however, Indo II scored a goal for Juventus, and then in the second half they sealed the win with a goal by Rogério. The first defeat of the competition meant that

Flamengo had to beat Corinthians, who had also lost to Juventus.

On 25 January, the most popular teams from Rio and São Paulo would contest one of the most famous matches of the competition. Flamengo had to proceed without Marcelinho, Marquinhos and Paulo Nunes for the match. Djalminha had a game for the ages, and on 15 minutes he assisted Nélio's goal. On 29 minutes his free kick went right down the middle for his second goal, and five minutes from the end of the first half, he converted a penalty for his hat-trick.

As if the second half could be any more fun, Flamengo poured on the hurt even more. Five minutes into the second, Djalminha hit a free kick that Piá headed in for a goal. On ten minutes, Wladimir then pulled one back for Corinthians, but this wasn't it, as Djalminha scored three more times. He converted a penalty on 17 minutes, headed in a crossed ball from the right on 34 and closed the scoring with a worldie almost from midfield. This was a 7-1 win and five goals from Djalminha.

Flamengo were through to the semi-finals four days later against Internacional, played in Suzano. Flamengo kept on the offensive, playing this time quick counter-attacks, opening in the first half in the 20th minute with a Luiz Antônio goal, then Djalminha scored a brace and Fabinho in the second half also got a brace. With all this firepower, the grand final on 31 January was a chance to avenge the loss to Juventus. All Flamengo needed was one goal, but it was an exquisite one from Júnior Baiano. Djalminha, already catching the eye of other clubs, served him with a magnificent pass, and Baiano, a defender by trade, ventured into the attack like a centre-forward, then beat the goalkeeper Alê with such a memorable touch. The party after the win was massive, with an Olympic lap and Djalminha lifting the trophy. The club would win more trophies before splitting players up by the mid-90s, mostly sold off at a bargain price, sometimes early to other Brazilian clubs. This lack of massive transfer deals would come to hurt the club later.

One was Djalminha, who just by his talent alone was going to be hard to keep. By 1993, he was off to São Paulo side Guarani. While he was there, they loaned him to J.League side Shimizu S-Pulse in 1994. That got him a move in 1996 to Palmeiras, where he continued to shine. In only 22 league matches, he hit 12 goals from central midfield. Djalminha was like other Brazilian players – he was about entertainment and giving the fans a show. This being the case, he was awarded the Bola de Ouro in 1996. This led to him being called up to the national team and eventually moving to Spain in 1997 and Deportivo La Coruña on a £10m transfer. His crowning achievement was Deportivo's 1999/2000 title season, when he scored ten goals in 31 games from the centre of midfield. In 2002, though, he headbutted Deportivo coach Irureta at the training ground, which ended his career in Europe and the national team.

On 10 December 1992, Luiz Augusto Beloso was elected president of Flamengo by the members, or the socios, for the following years. At 34, he was the youngest president in the club's history. Unfortunately, he also inherited a debt of one million dollars, back wages and structural problems. Most new presidents promise players or managers they are going to bring in; Beloso promised that he was going to bring in Renato Gaúcho for £450,000. This was key, because they needed talent for all three levels of competition: state, Copa de Brasil and the Copa Libertadores. Most of these fixtures were only 48 hours apart from each other.

Like in any season, players left, and a mini makeover was needed. Defender Wilson Gottardo, forwards Gaúcho, Djalminha and Adneri, and striker Nílson all left for other clubs. Júnior, a legend of the sport, and the last link to the 1981 team, retired at 39, though he was back, a month later, as the manager.

When Júnior came back in as manager, he started the season well, with wins over Cruzeiro, São Paulo, Botafogo and Internacional. In the Brazilian Cup, he powered them to the semi-finals, and in the Supercopa Libertadores they lost to São Paulo on penalty kicks 5-4. It then got worse for Flamengo, losing in the Brazilian league to Corinthians, Santos and Vitória. Then they lost in the Copa Rio to Vasco. This shows there have been some bad times for Flamengo in their history. Six major tournaments, four coaches, several transfers and no cup made it a very bad year. The debts were growing, and part of that was due to the country's inflation. The year 1994 would have to be very good to offset what had just happened for Flamengo.

The story of the bad times can make you appreciate the good times. Since the finances were in dire straits, more players had to leave: Renato Gaúcho, Edu Luma, Casagrande, Marcelinho, Júnior Baiano, Piá and Luiz Antônio. With not much money, the transfers were going to be very slim. They had to bring in players on loan like Carlos Alberto Dias, Charles Balano, Antonio Boladerio and Valdeir. The cost-cutting moves also meant that Flamengo had to blood some youth from the academy: Fabiano, Hugo, Magno and Sávio.

The bad times did not go away immediately. First, they had to play Grasshoppers from Switzerland, but lost 2-0. The form in the State Tournament was not that good, with draws against Bangu and Madureira. The local derbies didn't help much either: they lost to Vasco 3-1 and Fluminense 4-2, and drew with Botafogo 1-1. However, good times started to roll in quickly.

There was a 3-1 win against Fluminense, then another win over Botafogo, 3-1, and in a revenge match against Vasco, 2-1, both goals coming from new boy Charles Balano. Finally, Flamengo were able to put a line-up together: Gilmar, Charles Guerreiro, Marcos Adriano, Gelson, Rogério, Fabinho, Boiadeiro, Marquinhos, Belio, Charles Balano and Sávio. With this line-up, they won the first three matches in the State Cup and the Guanabara Cup. Then the machine that is normally Flamengo started to steamroll the league, beating Botafogo 7-1, followed by wins against Alvinegro and Fluminense, and a draw against Vasco.

World Cups are a very important thing in Brazil, so the national team had a send-off tour that took Gilmar out of the side for a while. Flamengo did not take that time off; in fact, they played a barnstorming domestic tour, playing 11 friendlies in nine Brazilian states. They went from Santa Catarina to Rondônia, from Piauí to Paraná. The club were finally able to buy some players: Dunga, Mauro Galvão and Júlio César. Marquinhos almost left for São Paulo, but Flamengo put a stop to that.

Flamengo renewed their relationship with a legend in 1994 as well. Zico was playing with Kashima Antlers, and the great man was getting his testimonial in Japan against his boyhood team, Flamengo. While in the orient, Flamengo took part in a tournament in Malaysia with many of the top clubs from around the world: Dundee United, Bayern Munich and Leeds United. The side that went into that tournament on 16 July 1994 was Adriano or Fábio Noronha in goal, Gelson, Rogério, Fabiano, Fabinho, Marquinhos, Sávio, Fábio Baiano, Hugo, Rodrigo Mendes and Magno.

Flamengo opened with a 1-1 draw with Dundee United, which put them through to play another United team in Leeds. This was a league-winning side for Leeds, having won the old English First Division a couple of seasons before, with David O'Leary, Gordon Strachan and Gary McAllister. Flamengo were able to grind out a 2-1 win for a shot at global super-club Bayern Munich. The German giants were hit big with World Cup players going off to the tournament.

There were some great players at the club: they had French striker Jean-Pierre Papin, Christian Ziege, Markus Babbel, Mehmet Scholl and Dietmar Hamann. On 3 July 1994, Flamengo played a simple 4-4-2 and it was a chippy match from the get-go. As the sport went into the new century, the play was still chippy and the players could get away with a lot more. Flamengo weren't the first to score – it was Papin who put the Bavarians ahead just before half-time. This put a fire in Flamengo when Rogério followed it up not much longer after with a shot past goalkeeper Uwe Gospodarek.

This really improved the morale of the side; now they knew they could play with the German giants. In the second half, Marquinhos put the ball in the back of the net on the half-hour mark for them to take the lead. To see off the match, Sávio ran down the left flank, outrunning everyone, to put in a sublime touch for the third and final goal. This was a good way to kick-start a new generation for Flamengo, and they came out of a difficult time and showed their toughness.

A lot of great players turned out for Flamengo as the 90s rolled on, even the enigmatic Romário. This was the same Romário who was rejected by Vasco da Gama as a 15-year-old for being too small; he only reached 5ft 5in as an adult. Because of this rejection, and the sweary rant afterwards, Romário made it his point to seek attention. Eventually, he did play for Vasco, which in turn got him into the youth system of the national team. Once he had made it to Vasco's senior team, he never looked back. In his three years, he scored 80 goals, and won two consecutive national titles. Once he became a prospect to watch, he was off to Europe and PSV Eindhoven. When he arrived, it was the season after the greatest season in PSV's history, the treble of 1988. Frank Arnesen, Eric Gerets and Wim Kieft scored 117 goals under the attacking brand of Guus Hiddink. They won the league, the Dutch Cup and the European Cup over Benfica. In his debut year, they clinched the double, and they would also get three league titles out of his four years. Romário also led the league in scoring for three years.

Eventually, he made his way to La Liga with Barcelona. As with anywhere he was, he wore out his welcome, and eventually in 1997 he made his way back to Rio, suiting up this time for Flamengo. This is where he comes into this story. Romário came from Barcelona after falling out with Johan Cruyff, in 1995/96, and it was the least productive of his two spells at the club – in 19 matches he only scored eight goals. He went back to Spain in 1996 for a bit, but ended up returning again to put himself in the best possible position for the France 1998 World Cup squad to defend the Brazilian title won four years before.

One of the bigger matches during Romário's time back in Rio with Flamengo was the match with Universidad de Chile on 6 October 1999 in the Mercosur Cup. This was one of the precursors to the Copa Sudamericana and the basic rules were the same. It involved the prominent clubs of South America, and it was a way to bring more money into clubs. Flamengo played against Universidad de Chile and won 7-0 in the group stages. Caio got the goals going in the fifth minute, then Romário scored four, and Mario Antonio and Rodrigo Mendes completed the seven goals.

In 1999 they had to play the Mercosur Cup, and they had to face countless trials to vanquish their own ghosts throughout the season. There were strange match-ups, great battles and internal struggles. This campaign had everything for a Hollywood movie but the turn of the century was a different year for a lot of people. A goal from forward Lê against Palmeiras in the middle of Parque Antártica ended the suffering the Flamengo fans had endured over the years against this side.

In 1997 CONMEBOL ended the Libertadores Super Cup, a tournament only nine years old. It was one that in 1988 brought all the champions on the continent. In its place, two new championships were introduced: the Mercosur Cup and the Merconorte Cup (involving clubs from further north of South America including North and Central America). The extinct tournament was the starting point for the Mercosur Cup, and they basically created a Superliga Cup. A generous financial contribution from television revenue was raised through the marketing company Traffic.

In all, 20 clubs from Argentina, Brazil, Chile, Paraguay and Uruguay were invited to compete in the competition. Seven clubs from Brazil were part of the tournament:

Corinthians, Cruzeiro, Flamengo, Grêmio, Palmeiras, São Paulo and Vasco. In the group phase the teams were divided into five groups of four, the winners of each bracket plus the top three runners-up advancing to the quarters. In the first edition, Flamengo reached the last round, where they lost 3-0 to Boca Juniors at La Bombonera, which eliminated them. The following year, Flamengo arrived with the Carioca title and started an era of winning.

Romário was the star of the team, led by manager Carlinhos. He had with him Luis Alberto, Athirson, goalkeeper Clemer, Pimentel, Célio Silva, Leandro Ávila, Beto, Leandro Machado and Caio. Flamengo were drawn into a good group with Olimpia, Colo-Colo and Universidad de Chile. The aim was to win it all and get the prize money that the club needed. The first match would come at the Maracanã on 27 July.

Flamengo came into the tournament with a mixed bag of results, winning in the final match of the Carioca Championship 1-0 over Grêmio. They played a match for a Campinas team and the play was not good. However, in the match against Olimpia, they opened with a 2-0 first-half scoreline, through goals from Romário. In the second half, Olimpia scored a penalty kick from Avalos to make it 2-1 in the end.

A week later in Santiago, Chile, at the Monumental Stadium, Flamengo had another huge offensive output. In the first half, Rodrigo Mendes got a brace with his two goals on 11 and 41 minutes, and, on 21, Romário contributed his normal goal of the game. To complete the rout at 4-0, Fabão beat Arbiza one on one. This put Flamengo top of the leaderboard, and they could wait for the next round which would be against Universidad de Chile back in Santiago.

Between the matches, Flamengo moved into the Brazilian Championship, where they won all three matches: Inter at Beira-Rio, Coritiba at the Maracanã and Sport at Ilha do Retiro. But that didn't help, as they went down on the sword to Universidad by a 2-0 scoreline.

In the Brazilian National Tournament, the pain kept coming as they lost to Grêmio at the Maracanã 4-3, but they won over Corinthians 2-1 and routed Botafogo 4-1 in São Paulo. They had to fly back to the Paraguayan capital where the strong winds rocked the plane into the city. On the field, the play got worse, as Leonardo Inacio scored an own goal in the 14th minute. Olimpia then had Esteche, and Franco made the score 2-1. Then in the second half, it got worse for the team in red and black. Just after two minutes, Luis Alberto stopped an Avalos ball with his arm, and the Paraguayans provoked him into getting expelled from the match. On 15 minutes Athirson was given a red card after a strong tackle. While that would get most teams down, Flamengo pushed ahead with Leandro Machado going for goal, to only have it ruled out for offside. With all of this, Olimpia ended up winning, complicating Flamengo's life. Colo-Colo and Olimpia both winning relegated Flamengo to third.

Between the loss in Asunción and the match against Cacique at the Maracanã, striker Caio made the headlines having to play as goalkeeper after Clemer was shown the red card in a 1-1 draw against Gama in Brasília, and then scoring the winning goal over São Paulo. This good run of form gained the vote of confidence from the manager Carlinhos. This kept Caio in the starting line-up even after Romário's return from suspension, with Leandro Machado going to the bench for the Colo-Colo match.

Caio would open the scoring, taking advantage of a loose ball by goalkeeper Arbiza. Near the end of the first half, Marco Antonio made a move past Rodrigo Mendes and put the ball in the back of the net for 2-0. In the second half, Flamengo had many opportunities to kill off the game, but they all went awry. Caio headed a ball past Arbiza but over the crossbar, and Romário wasted two chances one on one with Arbiza. Flamengo were punished for all their misses, as Colo-Colo charged back with goals from Muñoz and Vergara for the draw.

Flamengo were still in third place with seven points, and needed a miracle to qualify for the quarters. They couldn't even play for a draw; in fact, to keep their progress in their hands, the team needed to blow out a team by at least four goals. A more normal victory would force them to root for a draw in the match between Olimpia and Colo-Colo, or Boca Juniors to slip up. The Buenos Aires team were one of the main competitors for second-placed spots. Basically, all Flamengo had to do was hand Universidad de Chile one of the most humiliating losses they could possibly manage.

In order for this to happen, Carlinhos had to change the team completely: Robson replaced Clemer in goal, Maurinho was in at right-back, Juan took Fábio's place in defence and defensive midfielder Marcelo Rosa was in. Only Leandro Ávila was left in with Fábio Baiano and Beto setting up for Caio, Romário and Leandro Machado. They were looser and more flexible. The goal difference swung in the first half, as Flamengo supporters would expect their team to do.

After this great match, one would have hoped that the form would continue. For the most part, it did. The club trashed Vitória at the Maracanã 5-2, but the team added just one more point in the next six games and fell down the Brazilian National Tournament table. They did win again a month later over Bahia, and against Portuguesa 3-2.

The next opponent was Independiente, the club who beat them in the 1995 Super Cup, which still stung for the Flamengo fans. The two legs of the match would be played in the same week. In the first leg, on a Tuesday night in Avellaneda, Flamengo pulled off a great result. Reinaldo and Beto were shown red cards, but they managed to start scoring in spite of these two players' misdemeanours with a goal from Fábio Baiano after a pass from Romário. Calderón, on 32 minutes, drew Independiente level with Flamengo. Clemer, back in goal, saved Flamengo's skin.

On a rainy Friday night on 5 November, 36,257 at the Maracanã saw a great match in the semi-finals of the Mercosur. Athirson crossed from the left to Leandro Machado, who scored a goal with his head 16 minutes in. Then in the 20th minute, there was a midfield screamer that surprised goalkeeper Pontiroli for 2-0. Four minutes later, Leandro Machado sent a long pass into Romário, who was racing past defender Peñna at the edge of the area, and he made it 3-0. In the second half, the fourth goal came on 11 minutes when Romário sent it to Marcelo Rosa on the right wing, who crossed it on to Leandro Machado's head for his second goal.

Romário was always known for his partying; it was one of his undoings at PSV. After the 3-1 defeat by Juventude in the last round, Flamengo would participate in the Brazilian National Tournament, and they were eliminated from it. Romário and four players who left the team hotel were caught out on the town by the newspapers. Maurinho and Marcelo Rosa received light punishments, of which there isn't a record. Leandro Machado and Fábio Baiano were repeat offenders and were dropped from the team for a time. Romário had his contract terminated during this spell in Rio. In the days that followed, Flamengo fell to Internacional 1-0 and had a 1-1 draw.

To make matters worse, Flamengo were in the semi-finals of the Mercosur Cup, against a South American powerhouse in Peñarol. The last time the clubs had met was in 1982 in the semi-finals of the Libertadores with Zico still in the side. Peñarol won 1-0, on route to their next Libertadores title. Peñarol's path to the semi-finals of the Mercosur Cup was through hated rival Nacional, Vasco and Cerro Porteño in the group stage. They beat Olimpia in the quarters to reach the semi-finals. The only player of real substance in the Peñarol side was midfielder Pablo Bengoechea.

So Peñarol had to rely on being a physical team, and on that point, defensive midfielder De Souza committed two tough tackles in a row in the 22nd minute of play. The fouls earned him a direct expulsion, taking Peñarol down to ten men. This was the ignition that Flamengo needed, and in the 26th minute Leandro Machado scored from a penalty. On the 44-minute mark, after a short corner kick, Athirson ran into the area, passed it to Machado, and he found Maurinho's foot for the second goal of the half. In the second half, another player from the academy, Lé, scored the third goal in the 36th minute. The resounding victory served as a good way to win the fans back, and they hoped to have a less painful end of the season.

The second leg was in the Centenario stadium in Montevideo. Flamengo managed in the first half to keep a goalless draw, until stoppage time hit. Bengoechea took a perfect free kick for the opening goal of the game. After the half-time break, Leandro Machado had a free kick stopped by Flores, and Leonardo Inacio saw his free kick hit the crossbar, and the rebound was pushed away from the goalmouth.

Flamengo levelled the match in the 25th minute. Reinaldo ran down the left wing, venturing into the box, and was brought down by Cafu. Penalty! Athirson converted, without giving Peñarol goalkeeper Flores a chance. In another speedy counter-attack, Reinaldo fired home the second goal from midfield that stunned Flores. Flamengo had a four-goal advantage on aggregate, and their place in the final was assured. However, Peñarol did come back with a shot from García in the second half.

Now, with that ghost of the past vanquished, the foe in the final was Palmeiras. They had inflicted a painful loss in the Copa do Brasil, after a 2-1 first-leg scoreline at the Maracanã earlier in the year. Palmeiras came back in the second leg to win 4-2. Palmeiras were also much stronger than Flamengo, as they were backed by dairy company Parmalat, and had a massive squad full of national-team names. They had Júnior Baiano, Zinho and Paulo Nunes, who had helped them win the 1998 version of the Mercosur Cup, and the 1999 Copa Libertadores. The manager behind this great side was Luiz Felipe Scolari, a well-known name for Flamengo fans from when he was at Grêmio. His defensive midfielder, Dinho, kicked Sávio during the whole match.

The more things change, the more things stay the same. Peñarol being a thorn in the side of Flamengo was one of them. They swept Flamengo out of the 1982 Libertadores, stopping the golden era from winning back-to-back titles.

Peñarol were a big name in the Libertadores, but by the end of the 90s, Uruguayan football was in a low moment. At this point in the Libertadores, they had got to the semi-finals, going through against bitter rivals Nacional, Vasco and Cerro Porteño. They also beat Olimpia, to meet Flamengo again.

Peñarol were a dirty side, and it was not surprising that defensive midfielder De Souza had committed two bad fouls by the 22nd minute and was red-carded. With the man advantage, Flamengo took off. Four minutes later, a penalty kick was scored by Leandro Machado. Right before half-time, a short corner made it to Athirson's foot, and he passed it to Leandro Machado, who sent it to Maurinho for the second goal.

In the second half, Lê, who was from the academy, scored the third goal with a strong free kick. Flamengo were not done creating goals from there. Caio's header hit the bottom of the post but stayed out, and Reinaldo's follow-up was saved. This was enough to make the supporters feel good about the team. There were still battles to be won, and the return match was going to be one of them.

Flamengo spent most of the first half defending their scoreline. In stoppage time of the first half, Bengoechea's free kick opened the scoring for Peñarol. After the break, Flamengo reacted with a strong free kick from Leandro Machado that Flores saved, and Leonardo Inacio's free kick hit the crossbar. Marcelo Rosa's rebound was also saved. The equaliser came from Cafu fouling Reinaldo in the area, and Athirson converted the penalty kick. With yet another counter-attack, Reinaldo finally got his first goal as a professional. Now, Flamengo had four goals on aggregate and the spot in the final was approaching.

Peñarol pulled one back in the 33rd minute through García. In stoppage time, a phantom penalty by Maurinho on Dario Rodriquez was converted by Bengoechea. It gave the Uruguayans the victory but did not stop Flamengo from moving on. Peñarol did not like how they were eliminated and wanted to redeem their honour. They decided to throw punches and kicks that looked as if they were from a battle. Eventually, the police had to break up the ruckus. Flamengo had to take refuge in the changing rooms. Ten players from Peñarol were suspended by CONMEBOL for anywhere from three to ten matches. The club were also fined and warned about the behaviour of the players. To add fuel to the fire, Bengoechea had excessive levels of caffeine in his system.

This wasn't, however, a great Flamengo side; it was made up of academy players, low-cost players from small clubs and a few veterans. Flamengo were better known at this point for their fighting spirit than their technical characteristics. Clearly, they were inferior to Palmeiras. Such was the underdog spirit of the team that the directors for the club doubted Carlinhos, that he could lead the team to a continental title, ending the 19-year drought. They didn't hide the fact they were looking to bring back 1981 manager Paulo César Carpegiani from São Paulo.

On 16 December the two sides played their first leg at the Maracanã, in front of only 13,414 fans. Carlinhos was willing to come out ahead in the first match, then play a cagey second match four days later in São Paulo. Flamengo lined up with Clemer in goal, Célio Silva and Juan as centre-halves, Maurinho and Athirson on the wings, Leandro Ávila, Marcelo Rosa, Iranildo and Leonardo Inacio in midfield, and Leandro Machado and Reinaldo up front.

Rodrigo Mendes and Vaio were on the bench. Palmeiras selected Marcos, Arce, Júnior Baiano, Galeano, Júnior, César Sampaio, Rogério, Alex, Zinho, Paulo Nunes and Oséas. Euller would come on during the second half.

In the first half, the Flamengo supporters were the ones who would celebrate early on. Within the first five minutes, Iranildo's corner from the right side was controlled by Maurinho, who sent it into Juan for the first goal, from a header. Palmeiras roared back in the last minute of the first half, when Júnior Baiano sent Clemer the wrong way with a penalty kick. It looked as though Palmeiras were going to take the match when 23 minutes into the second half they took the lead, when Asprilla beat Clemer with a header.

It has been foolish to count out Flamengo, and on 25 minutes Caio got on the end of a Leandro Machado header for 2-2. Just catching their breath, Flamengo had to defend a ball sent in from Asprilla into Paulo Nunes for 3-2. The frenetic pace kept up as Caio received a pass on the edge of the area and hit a low ball into the back of the net for 3-3. The game would only see a winner in the 38th minute, as Reinaldo headed in a cross from Athirson to seal the win 4-3.

Four days later, on 20 December, a crowded Antartica Park was ready to see what Flamengo had for their home team. The only change for Flamengo was Caio in Iranildo's place. Palmeiras needed a win to force a third-match play-off, and they came in with a more offensive set-up, with Euller and Asprilla replacing Rogério and Oséas. The mostly home crowd cheered on Alviverde, when he put Palmeiras into the lead in the 19th minute. Júnior conceded a penalty on Leandro Machado, which Arce converted.

In the first half, Asprilla hit Athirson with an elbow, which was ignored by referee Luciano Almeida and his assistant. Little by little, Flamengo came closer to equalising just before the break. Into the second half, the equalising goal would come, as Rodrigo Mendes shot at goal. It was pushed away by Marcos, but the rebound was snatched upon by Caio for 2-1. Not too much later, Rodrigo, with a clever move, beat Marcos for 2-2. But Arce then put one past Clemer for 3-2. It looked again like the tide had turned in favour of Palmeiras.

Then the football Gods smiled on Flamengo as Lé, the young academy player, got his foot on the ball and put in the winning goal in the 83rd minute. The aggregate score of 7-6 was good enough for the first Continental Cup in 18 years. The grit and determination of the side to make them winners again is something, even well over 20 years later, that is still remembered.

Not all great players who turned out for Flamengo came from Rio or the Southern Hemisphere. Such is the case with Serbian player Dejan Petković who, in the twilight of his career, spent time in Rio. Players live to win titles, and in Dejan's case he didn't have to play the best game to win a title. It was the first Brazilian title for the club in 17 years, and all Dejan had to do was set up a corner for Ronaldo Angelim's winning goal over Grêmio for the 2-1 win. Flamengo were in 14th place when Dejan signed with the club for the second time, and he made a massive impact on his arrival.

His first chance with Flamengo came in 2001, and it looked like another stop along a journeyman career, which had seen the heights of playing with Red Star Belgrade and in Spain. In the 2001 Campeonato Carioca against Vasco da Gama at the Maracanã, in the 88th minute of the second leg with a 3-3 scoreline on aggregate, Dejan delivered a perfect free kick to win the match. That sent him into the minds of Flamengo fans as an idol, even though temporarily in 2002 he left for the city rivals Vasco. There, he won the 2003 Carioca, before moving yet again to Shanghai Shenhua for big bucks. Dejan made another sojourn to Vasco to save them from relegation, before leaving for Al-Ittihad and big money.

After that profitable period in the middle of the noughties, he returned to Brazil and became somewhat of a journeyman, playing for many clubs: Fluminense, Goiás, Santos and Atlético Mineiro in a period between 2005 and 2009. At this point, he arrived back at his true home Flamengo, and the Maracanã. The club still owed him money from his previous stint, a common theme for the club. To settle the debt, Dejan was reportedly promised 15 per cent of the home gate receipts, which the supporters did not like because of his age. However, he became an idol of the club and the sport in Brazil after winning the 2009 title with Flamengo. Dejan also saw out the rest of his career in Rio. He became the third foreigner inducted into the Maracanã Walk of Fame, along with Eusébio and Franz Beckenbauer. Dejan netted a total of 167 goals during his time in Brazil.

On the topic of the debt issues, these really wrecked the club. It started out as a great idea and just fell apart from there. At the end of 1999, the club was looking to kick off the next century with money in their pocket and world dominance again. They thought the solution was a saviour from Switzerland. At a ceremony in Gávea, Swede Heinz Schurtenberger, representing ISL, stated that the agreement between ISL and Flamengo would make Flamengo Brazil's number one club in business, and one of the most successful clubs in the world. The agreement was for 15 years, and was worth 80 million dollars at the time. Around 40 million would be used to invest in football, and it provided the construction of a stadium. In addition to all of this, they would be able to purchase where the team trained.

The Flamengo fans were optimistic, dreaming of players like Batistuta, Seedorf and Rincón. At the beginning, the only name was Petković, and then eventually players like Tuta, Catê, Jorge Soto and Lúcio arrived. Even more came later like Martingale, Alex, Denílson and Edílson. The results did not come fast, salary delays started and then the dreaded administrative problems arose. The club were going down with the money.

After 15 months, in April of 2001 the partnership ended. ISL, which was delaying payments to the club, was declared bankrupt in Switzerland, and Flamengo were left with debts. The club's budget was cut almost in half, and it got worse from there. On 9 July 2002, Flamengo president Edmundo Santos Silva was impeached, which was a first in the club's history. He was accused of administrative impropriety. Flamengo went through a few bad years of financial crunch before recovering by 2011.

The 2009 Campeonato Brasileiro Série A title is another one of those singular moments in Flamengo history which points out why they are the best-supported club in Brazil. It was also the redemption story of Adriano for the people. Deep personal problems had forced him to leave Italy for a new club; once he had found a new club, he had arrived on the shores of Rio de Janeiro and Flamengo. In the noughties, many of the top players in Brazil were playing in Europe, making the standard of play very poor. Adriano was a hulk of a man, and most of the time he made it look like an adult playing a child's game. Any decent cross into him would result in a goal either off his head or his left foot.

Adriano came back to a club which he had risen through the ranks at from the academy. The fans were cheering him but forgot that before he had left in 2001 for Italy, supporters hated him. At 17 years old, Brazilian national-team manager Émerson Leão thought a lot of him and handed him an international debut in a World Cup qualifier against Colombia in November 2000. Adriano, a few months later in Ecuador in the South American Under-20 Championship, looked even better. But when he played for Flamengo, he could not get the service he needed.

However, when he came back, he got great service down the right flank from Leonardo Moura. Adriano was a more complete player and could play the middle of the pitch with his team-mates. He was also lucky enough to link up with Dejan Petković, and all this team needed was to beat old foe Grêmio to clinch the title. Petković struggled in the match, and with it level at 1-1 in the 80th minute, he was about to be replaced. The substitute board was up, and the new player was going on at the next break.

At that point, Flamengo had won a corner, and Petković was a corner-kick specialist. He curled the ball in from the left, allowing centre-back Ronaldo Angelim to put it in the back of the net for the title. This was not the first time Petković and Adriano had played together in Rio; in fact, both were on their second tour with the club. They had played together nine years before at the start of the 2000s. On this tour, they struck up an instant rapport, Petković operating from the left midfield while rotating with support striker Zé Roberto. Petković carved up defences on a weekly basis, while Adriano applied the finishing touch. Flamengo were 14th after 21 of the 38 matches played in 2009. Then they took fire, as many Flamengo sides had, over the final 17 matches – the club won 12, losing only once before winning the title.

For this to happen, they had to have the great players above. Flamengo's winning total of 67 points was the lowest number of points for a winner since 2003. Reasons for this were the strength of the Brazilian Série A, and the Brazilian currency being so strong. Big-name players like Adriano came back from Europe. The National Tournament could always be counted on for some surprising moments. Ronaldo and Corinthians won the Brazilian Cup in mid-season, qualifying them for the 2010 Copa Libertadores, but their form disappeared after the cup win.

Flamengo's form over the last couple of months made them worthy champions. Like with any title-winning team, hindsight is on full display, and if any of the top clubs had played up to their level, it would have been a different story. Though in Flamengo's defence, not many clubs, outside of Corinthians with Ronaldo, had a Adriano or Petković. But they were not the last great players before the Copa Libertadores to play for the Rio club.

It was a bad year for the club in 2005, and as it got to the end of the season, they were a candidate to go down. This would have been a first for them. It took a win in the 40th round of the Brazilian Championship for them to stay up. On 20 November against Paraná at Pinheirão, the club secured safety with a 1-0 win for the 51 points they needed to stay up. Flamengo dominated most of the play in the first half, getting enough chances to score. On 11 minutes, Renato crossed to Diego Souza, who got around the defence and sent the ball towards goal, but it hit the crossbar. Eight minutes later, Leonardo Moura missed a sitter to put points on the board.

Paraná only threatened danger in the 36th minute as Borges was in the area but the ball ended up in Flamengo goalkeeper Diego's hands. The second half started out the same, with Renato's free kick on ten minutes hitting the post after a deflection from Paraná goalkeeper Flávo's hands. Flamengo had another great opportunity in the 42nd minute from Obina. Fortunately, he redeemed himself in the 47th minute, hitting a goal from a cross from the edge of the area for 1-0. The ghost of relegation moved away from Flamengo for the first time.

One of the best times after coming out of the debt debacle was when Ronaldinho came to Rio. Ronaldinho was one of the best players in the 21st century in Europe, but like many, when his European adventure was up, he came back to Brazil. There was a memorable match between Flamengo and Neymar's Santos on 27 July 2007 that could have been the passing of the torch.

Only a month had passed since Santos had lifted the Copa Libertadores over Flamengo's foe Peñarol. Santos were still basking in the glory of the cup for the third time in their history. On the other side, Flamengo were dreaming of winning another Brazilian title, as they were undefeated after 11 matches in the Brasileirão, having won five and drawn six. Outside of Neymar and Ronaldinho meeting for the first time in club play, two of the best managers of the time were meeting again: Muricy Ramalho at Santos and Vanderlei Luxemburgo at Flamengo.

At the time, Santos were at the wrong end of the table, sitting in 13th place. With Flamengo's great run, they were third and moving up. Flamengo's title hopes were laying on the whim of the maverick midfielder Ronaldinho. Both lined up a little before 10pm as André Luiz de Freitas Castro blew his whistle to get the match going. It started off with Santos running all over Flamengo in the open field. Flamengo's players weren't going to let Santos just dictate the match, so they fouled Neymar after he received a pass from Ganso.

On four minutes in, Ronaldinho's back-heel pass to Deivid was fumbled, creating a counter-attack for Santos. Neymar got the green light to pull off the first showboating moment of the match, playing it in for ex-Manchester City player Elano, who was on his second of three tours with Santos. Elano then, with his exquisite passing, left it for Borges to go one on one with Flamengo goalkeeper Felipe for the 1-0 lead.

Flamengo needed to react or the match could get out of hand fast. Ronaldinho missed on far less passes, created opportunities and controlled the match. So much of this opening part of the match for Flamengo was Ronaldinho, and he almost scored on two occasions. His shot in the 11th minute missed to the right of Rafael's goal, and on 15 minutes he fired a weak shot at the goal, which was easily collected. Despite Flamengo's best efforts, Santos were the ones who scored next, with Neymar laying on the ground and touching the ball to Borges for 2-0.

Deivid had a chance to open the scoring, with an open goal in front of him, but just managed to miss it. The ball hit the shin of the Santos keeper, hit the crossbar and went out. A move like this at any level would be humiliating for anyone. With the 11-game unbeaten streak on the line, Santos made it more nerving for the Flamengo fans. The third goal was picked as FIFA's most beautiful goal of the year, but 3-0 was harsh. Neymar in the middle of the pitch passed it to Borges, who put it in the air, returning it to Neymar, who was one on one with Flamengo defensive duo Welinton and Ronaldo Angelim, and he then saw Felipe. Neymar's final touch was elegant, light and under the reach of Vila Belmiro for the third goal.

Flamengo tend to take shots to the ego in their stride, and beat them. They came back with two quick goals, one by Ronaldinho and one from Thiago Neves. This put the pressure back on Santos, who had their defensive flaws. In the second half, Flamengo kept it on through a great sequence of passing between Deivid, Léo Moura and Thiago Neves. Eventually, Deivid got his head on it for 3-3.

Neymar was not done, and on the 40-minute mark he left everyone in his wake and got into the penalty area. As something that was to become a trick that he would use many times, he fell down in the area, drawing a foul on Williams for a penalty and a yellow card. Elano took the penalty, scoring while attempting the Panenka. Ronaldinho, ever the showman, made sure Flamengo would win, but being down 4-3 was not optimal. He was always a game-changing genius, and he surprised everyone with a historic moment, hitting a low free kick under the wall for 4-4. Game on!

The match kept being busy. Santos had the genius of Neymar to rely on, and he launched a counter-attack from the right, dribbling towards Leonardo Moura, and he fell down in the penalty area again. The referee saw through the simulation, only awarding a corner, and the fouling in the area got a little extreme with Renato Abreu getting a yellow card. Neymar, in the 29th minute of the second half, had another shot on goal that was turned away. A great match like this needed a winner, and that came on 36 minutes, when a mistake by Ganso found the feet of Deivid, who passed it on to Thiago Neves. Neves found Ronaldinho invading the penalty area for the 5-4 goal.

There was still time on the clock, and no one gave up. Ronaldinho looked to have another goal, the sixth. However, he missed the post. Neymar, not much better, lost his cool and got a yellow card. In stoppage time, Ronaldinho was fouled, but still played the ball into Thiago Neves as it looked like Flamengo wanted the sixth goal. But the referee whistled for the end of the match, and the Flamengo players received a standing ovation at the Vila Belmiro. Time machines are not a thing, but in this era of cameras everywhere and YouTube, matches can be seen many times over. Given the opportunity, watch this match as it has become a classic one has to see.

Not everything that happens at Flamengo is good. On 8 February 2019 there was a fire in a makeshift dormitory that killed ten young kids who were on youth terms. Nothing good has come out of this. On the one-year anniversary, the Flamengo players and staff paid tribute to the boys while at the training ground. The family and relatives were barred by a security barrier to get close to the site, so they knelt in prayer by the side of the road. Flamengo were rightfully blasted in their response to the tragedy.

The fire took the lives of Christian Esmerio, Jorge Eduardo, Athila Paixao, Rykelmo Vianna, Arthur Vinicius de Barros Sailva Freitas, Bernardo Pisetta, Samuel Thomas Rosa, Pablo Henrique, Vitor Isaias and Gedson Santos. To add insult to injury, only three of the families reached compensation agreements with Flamengo, and nobody was held responsible for the fire until January 2021. Like with the crumbling stadiums in England, the club was warned of the safety problems of the dormitories. It was a horrendous scene; the boys were sleeping in shipping containers back to back, the exits barred except one.

The site had only been granted planning permission for a car park, and the Rio local government fined Flamengo 31 times for a lack of a safety certificate. The fire started when an air-conditioning unit short-circuited, the fire spreading quickly through the insulating foam used for the construction. Luckily, 16 kids got out alive, but the ones that died couldn't even get out. The Rio de Janeiro state prosecutors suggested an out-of-court settlement, which was an immediate payment of £355,000 to each family, plus Flamengo paying £1,750 per month to each family until the day their sons would have turned 45. Flamengo had the money to cover it annually; in 2019, before the COVID pandemic, the club brought in £152 million. They instead started to barter with the families, which should be considered shameful.

Three of the families have reached settlements with the club, and there is a confidentiality agreement in place with a fine if they break the deal. December 2019 the club was ordered to pay the remaining families until the case was resolved. The club, after immediately appealing the order, eventually fulfilled it, reluctantly. This is how enemies are treated, not, for a lack of better words, employees of your club. Flamengo have been criticised worldwide, both in the media and online.

Chapter 11

2019, Jorge Jesus, Liverpool, COVID

WHILE THE 1980s was a great time for Flamengo, 30 years later the club had another great era. However, in 2020/21 there was a pandemic worldwide. Life became very polarised and it isolated people from their families. Football tried to keep itself going during COVID.

Before the world shut down, Liverpool and Flamengo met again in the newer version of the Intercontinental Cup. The Intercontinental Cup merged with the Club World Cup in 2004 for a one-off game between the winner of the two hemispheres. Liverpool were just emerging on to their next great spell, with Jürgen Klopp in charge of his great side. They were coming off winning the Champions League, after losing out in the final the year before. Liverpool met Flamengo in Japan on 21 December 2019 and finally got their revenge on them by winning 1-0 through Brazilian Roberto Firmino. It was also one of the few titles which Liverpool had never won. Flamengo were already on a Brasilieirao Serie A title and Copa Libertadores double.

Portuguese manager Jorge Jesus came in before the 2019 season, and made the club great again. He likes to be called Mister, and came as an outsider from Europe. It's a unique thing that a manager from outside the continent came to Brazil with the pedigree that he had. He had a star-studded cast and needed to mould the team into a powerful side. Jorge Jesus's quality as a coach have never been in question. He did amazing work in both Saudi Arabia and Portugal.

The key question was how he was going to adapt to playing in Brazil. There were many differences: the pitches are different, the weather south of the equator prevents high-intensity games; as we mentioned, the Brazilian football calendar is insane and the atmosphere isn't as strict. Flamengo supporters are some of the most demanding in Brazil, but Jorge Jesus had managed at Benfica so that was a good point in his favour.

The formation varies a lot, but that's par for the course for most fluid, flexible managers. Jorge Jesus was known for using the 4-1-3-2, but he only used it in his early matches in Brazil. The most common formation used by Jesus at Flamengo was the 4-4-2, with two players in the middle, and two wingers with the freedom to move inwards towards the centre of the pitch. The pair up top were Bruno Henrique and Gabigol. When the 4-2-3-1 was used, Éverton Ribeiro was more central and Bruno Henrique was to the right. The players picked up their movements and roles very fast.

In the offensive build-up of a match, Flamengo's attack was labelled as upright. The percentage of possession in matches could be very high, but they weren't for long possession or passing just to pass. It was about possession with purpose, taking the advantage on the field with a controlling nature, and speed in building attacks. The speed and movement of Gabigol with Bruno Henrique running alongside built the depth of the attack. There were also the coordination between Éverton Ribeiro and Gerson, the versatility of William Arão and the deadliness of De Arrascaeta.

Defence was also a key to Jorge Jesus's tactics. Rodrigo Caio and Pablo Marí were centre-backs who could make great passes. The ball was played well from the first time it was kicked. Filipe Luis and Rafinha were the wingers/full-backs. They occupied the flanks, dictating the rhythm of the team with their experience at high levels in their careers. The goal-kick routines were devastating, with three players lined up. Wiliam Arão pushed forward past the centre-backs, freeing up Rafinha and Filipe Luis who occupied the flanks. That spread out the opposition defence for the team to move the ball. Pushing forward, Gérson was distributed to players floating around, like Éverton Ribeiro and De Arrascaeta. From there, they had the attacking duo of Bruno Henrique and Gabigol in the final third.

Even though we just touched on the defence briefly, for organisation Flamengo used zonal marking. The wingers tended to follow their opposite number from time to time, but were in predetermined areas. Flamengo positioned themselves with close lines between the defence and the midfield. The Flamengo players' defensive intensity picked up when they were defending their zone. This led to them scoring lots of goals from counter-attacks, because Flamengo were lethal when they had room to run. Gabigol, Bruno Henrique and De Arrascaeta were all cut out for playing on the counter. Flamengo have conceded very few goals on rival counter-attacks. The club took this play very far; while it wasn't the glory period of the 1980s, Flamengo made their play much better than it had been.

The 2019 final was going to be normal despite the main issues off the pitch. The year before was the Super Final between Boca Juniors and River Plate. The violence leading up to the match the previous year made CONMEBOL move the match to Real Madrid's Santiago Bernabeu stadium. The incident was another bad mark on South American football. River fans pelted the Boca team bus with objects, midfielder Pablo Pérez sustaining an eye injury, and the whole Boca squad suffered the effects of the tear gas the police had to use to disperse the crowd. Keeping the match in the Southern Hemisphere was going to be tricky, and moving it to the Spanish capital was criticised. Sadly, so much of the sport is about extracting money from the poor by the wealthy.

For the first time in history, the 2019 Libertadores Final would be played as a one-legged game in a neutral venue, a lot like the Champions and Europa League finals. Traditionally, finals in South America have been a two-legged, home and away affair. South America is massive; the whole of Europe without Russia could fit comfortably into Brazil. Travel is hard and expensive in South America. Mass migration for a single match is even harder, even for the wealthiest people.

A one-legged final is viewed as a way to make it a more attractive proposition for casual fans. Supporters and pundits scoffed at the pandering move, as following the sport is not as hard as people tend to think it is. Like with anything in CONMEBOL, the location of the final was changed at the last minute, meaning people who had made the trip or reservations were out of pocket for the money they had spent. The match was originally scheduled for Santiago, but the political protests led CONMEBOL to move the final to Lima, Peru. Flamengo eventually got to play a fascinating match with River Plate, with their manager Marcelo Gallardo, a former player at the club, already in his fifth year at the club with two Copa Libertadores titles, a Copa Sudamericana and two Argentine Cups in his coaching career. Despite all of this, Flamengo won, and went on to the Club World Cup against familiar foe Liverpool.

Just days into 2020, COVID was spreading throughout the world and by February the globe was shutting down. This was all during the first couple of months of former federal deputy for Rio de Janeiro, Jair Bolsonaro's, first term as Brazilian president. Like with anything during this time, COVID was ravaging and closing down life. In fact, many football leagues shut down during this time, with the exception of the Belarusian league.

Even when society started to open back up, leagues were still not letting supporters back into stadiums. COVID as we have known in its truest form reached South America at the end of February of 2020. That was much later than the rest of the world. Then it exploded in the region; by 4 May there were hundreds of thousands of cases, and thousands of deaths. The hotspots, like with most countries, were the big metropolitan areas like São Paulo and Rio de Janeiro.

Of course, when you are talking about a country during crisis time, one has to look at how the leadership reacts to the situation. In that case, President Bolsonaro was attacked from all angles and all parts of the world. They perceived his lack of public or tangible results of the pandemic as problematic. Most of the world stuck to physical distancing, lockdowns and mask mandates. Instead of attacking the pandemic, he attacked the people criticising him. In April of 2020, he sacked health minister Luiz Henrique Mandetta for open criticism of Bolsonaro's actions.

The public health sector was already stretched thin at the beginning and needed a good hand at the top to help combat the problem. Worldwide, we were met with daily, sometimes hourly, updates on the death counts, and calls for auxiliary spaces for hospital beds for hotspots. The poor were hard hit because of living in shanty towns where hygiene, physical distancing and clean water wasn't possible. While people should have the choice to figure out life on their own, the Brazilian government didn't help their own.

That also doesn't account for the employment sector either, where large parts of society lost their jobs. That pushed more into the public healthcare system. In Brazil, you also have the massive problem of logging and mining in the Amazon rainforest. These people were bringing COVID into the mining communities, where the healthcare system was even more stretched. Just having the pandemic was bad, but Bolsonaro cut the science budget, and there were general cuts in public services and social security that didn't help either. So what had to happen was that organisations banded together to come up with solutions. The big takeaway from COVID was that governments, despite their money, and elections couldn't adapt to a worldwide problem when they didn't want to.

Citizens had to worry about themselves. And in that case, we saw online and via newscasts the hoarding of supplies. The global rush to buy toilet paper was broadcast everywhere, but it didn't stop there. In communities you saw people stocking up on everything. Shortly after that you saw companies and affiliates price gouging anything that was needed. After all, do not let a crisis go to waste. In America, we saw hand sanitiser get so scarce that alcohol companies had to start making it. Boxes of masks and stand-alone masks jumped up in price. In a time when people could be showing unity, greed came out.

The fear as people got into summer and autumn of 2020 was how to reopen society. While parts of the world did, in a way, 'soft' shutdowns, letting only essential businesses stay open, many areas of the world locked down tight, and hurt economies for the good of the people. The good was only to keep people from getting sick or dying. Control the spread. The 15 days to flatten the curve was brought up. But the opening up of society and how to do it was a key problem. How do we let people back into a world that has changed, for whatever reasons? Many opinions and theories were unleashed, along with the vaccines.

The recovery won't be even among all communities; it's going to be more of a K-shaped recovery. That's where some parts quickly recover and others continue to suffer. This really points to how each sector is governed and how the citizenry reacts to more government rule. The pandemic also showed the lengths to which the citizenry were willing to put up with the rules from the government. The willing and not willing had to be able to coexist. The hypocrisy of media and government officials telling people to follow the rules and then flaunting their blatant disregard for them was shown many times over.

The conversion back to a functioning society in Brazil has to account for world-class soccer, carnival and the rainforest. Brazil is 2.73 per cent[35] of the world's population, so to be able to turn back to having people in the stands would be a challenge to say the least. Players on the field, both at practice and during the games, were going to be the interesting aspect.

35_www.worldometers.info/world-population/brazil-
population/#:~:text=Brazil%20population%20is%20equivalent%20
to%202.73%25%20of%20the%20total%20world%20population

Across the rest of the world, we saw football leagues kick back up in early summer without any fans in 2020. For many fans, it hurt to see the games just on television. Liverpool in England won their first English Premier League title, and had to celebrate without fans or buses in the streets of Liverpool. Boca Juniors won the Argentine League going into the global shutdown, and the AFA waited for a long time to get them the championship trophy. By the time Major League Soccer had their title game, some fans were allowed into the stands to see the Columbus Crew win their title. Regions and leagues had to adapt to what they could do with respect to the rules they were given.

In Brazil, on the other hand, in normal times, the State Championship would be starting in January and February, generally going through to April. This wasn't a normal year. Some of the regional competitions were played, and a large majority of them were postponed. The 2021 Rio Grande de Norte championship was cancelled, just like the rest of the high-profile State Championships.

It made sense given how the pandemic had wrecked Brazil. So the clubs based in states enduring an emergency lockdown would have to relocate their fixtures to allow them to be played. The Campeonato Paulista was temporarily halted, and some of the fixtures that were able to be played were moved to Volta Redonda. Various clubs around the country scheduled games to be played in the Estádio Nacional de Brasilia Mané Garrincha in the Federal District. Those games included State Championships, CONMEBOL fixtures and the Brazilian Super Cup. The Brazilian Football Federation (CBF) pointed out that they wanted to keep the State Championships going so there wouldn't be a fixture congestion leading up to the national leagues. This was based on them saying they felt that the protocols were competent and safe for all attending the games. That didn't happen, as players kept testing positive for the virus, at an alarming rate.

So with that, the league season was all set to resume in late summer on 9 August, which was given the all-clear signal from the CBF. This was a return to whatever normal that people could muster at this point. While there will be strong opinions on coming back, the fans needed a break from the pain. Bolsonaro and Flamengo were making strong points for the return of soccer, but to get back, there would have to be steps taken before returning to the field.

Flamengo were the biggest club in the country and favourites to win the league again. This season, in the strangest of all strange seasons, the 2020 Flamengo side resembled the 2009 edition of Flamengo. For the final game of that season, they lined up in a 4-4-2. With Dejan Petković and Adriano, the club beat Grêmio at a packed Maracanã to top the table for the first time and win the title. In 2020, on the last day of the current campaign, the club won a title-deciding game against Internacional. It helped for the fans of the club to get some good news in.

The 2020 season was not the easiest for the club with COVID and injuries; they had to dig deep to follow up last year's quintuple. Flamengo rode so high with Jorge Jesus and to expect any further obstacles would be hard to imagine. The club would just deal with it and move on. It was going to be a challenge to rival what Jesus did, maybe borderline impossible. At the least, Flamengo fans demand a Brazilian title, and the run to a title is a marathon, not a sprint.

When Jesus returned to Portugal to manage Benfica, Pep Guardiola's former assistant manager Domènec Torrent came in. Torrent had spent some time as the New York City FC manager in the MLS. The Rio club wanted to have someone who had the same profile as Jesus, with a modern idea on how to play the game. However, Dom never really settled into the Brazilian game and left his post. Every loss was solely Torrent's responsibility, and that was running parallel with Jesus's 12-month-long victory parade. The fans and the media demand winning at all times, and under Torrent they could never get themselves going. So out he went, and in came Rogério Ceni, the former high-scoring goalkeeper who has had a nomadic coaching existence.

He had to restore the club back to the top. Towards the end of the season, it looked like the club was figuring out Ceni's tactics. William Arão played a more defensive role, Diego had space in the midfield and it all just clicked. They were supplemented by other great players from the 2019 season: striker Gabigol, attacking midfielder Éverton Ribeiro and Georgian De Arasecaeta. Bruno Henrique, who played so well against Liverpool in the Club World Cup match, became an even better player for the club during the season. Midfielder Gérson provided some great work for the rest of the team, and Pedro chipped away at matches with vital goals. This title didn't have the glamour of the 2019 title, but the club wouldn't have it any other way.

What was more significant to this was, for the first time since Zico's days in 1982 and 1983, Flamengo had won back-to-back titles. However, managing in Brazil is a fickle place – sometimes three or four managers come and go during the season. There were still doubts on Ceni and if he was the right man for the job, but he wasn't fired right away. The club and the sport as a whole needs more patience and sustainability.

Flamengo's debts grew to the hundreds of millions during the pandemic, which isn't a surprise as most big clubs around the world carry debt. In Brazil, clubs have to sell their young players to Europe to make a profit or have to transfer money for themselves. The club know that in the long run, it will all be fine. They have a fine squad, and the experience to win and dominate in the Brazilian game.

The race for the title seemed, at the end, a six-horse race. Slowly, each club fell away – Grêmio and Palmeiras fell away due to fixture pile-ups, São Paulo fell away under the pressure of trying to win their first title in years, Atlético Mineiro were brilliant at times but lacked the consistency and Internacional blew it at the end. Flamengo did not win the title by default; they were just there in the right place at the right time.

Flamengo took the home stretch of the season the way most champions would, winning five out of the last six games. The loss was a 2-1 game against São Paulo in the match that clinched the eighth title for the club. One of the wins along the way was a 4-1 victory in the 25th round against Santos at the Maracanã. Some matches with that many goals are very up and down, but in the first half, Flamengo only came away with a 1-0 lead after a rebounded shot by Gérson.

After the second-half restart, Arrascaeta was taken down in the box after two minutes. Up stepped Gabigol for the first of his brace on the day to go up 2-0. Sensing the pace of the game was on their side, Arrascaeta played the ball in from the left to Bruno Henrique, who crossed to João

Paulo, and he took a shot on the goal that missed. On the rebound, Filipe Luís hit it in for 3-0.

Then it turned from bad to worse for Santos, as 25 minutes into the second half, the Santos keeper fouled Éverton Ribeiro, which drew Gabigol to the penalty spot again. And sure enough, he hit it home for 4-0. Santos worked the ball into Bruninho, who headed in a consolation goal for the 4-1 final score. The Flamengo line-up was Diego Alves, Isla, Rodrigo Caio, Natan, Filipe Luís, João Gomes, Gérson (Pedro), Arrascaeta (Pepê), Éverton Ribeiro (Michael), Bruno Henrique (Vitinho) and Gabi (Pedro Rocha).

In the final round of the 2020 Brasileirão, Flamengo beat Internacional 2-1 on Sunday, 22 February 2021. And they took the lead in the championship for the first time all season. It was a cagey match, as in the first half, after 11 minutes, Internacional opened the scoring through Edenílson from the penalty spot to make it 1-0. The goal spurred the Flamengo side into attack and on to the front foot. However, Internacional were able to defend the attacks that Flamengo threw at them.

After 28 minutes, Filipe Luís passed the ball to Bruno Henrique on the left, who played a low ball into Arrascaeta for 1-1. But Flamengo weren't done with the scoring chances. In the 40th minute, Éverton Ribeiro shot from outside the area and it went towards the left side of the net past the goalkeeper, but over the goal. The first half ended with a 1-1 score.

In the second half, Rodinei got a red card after a hard tackle on Filipe Luís, so Rogério Ceni took off Isla and put on Pedro to make the formation more attacking to get the win. Arrascaeta ran up the middle of the field and laid off a sweet pass to Gabigol for the 2-1 win. Not to miss out on the scoring chances, in the 49th minute Bruno Henrique missed the goal with a good chance. The Flamengo line-up for this one was Hugo, Isla (Pedro), Rodrigo Caio (Natan), Gustavo Henrique, Filipe Luís, Diego (João Gomes), Gérson, Éverton Ribeiro, De Arrascaeta, Bruno Henrique and Gabi (João Lucas).

The monetary cost of COVID on the world game will rise into the billions after all the accounting is done by clubs. Generally, clubs generate between 40 and 45 billion US dollars annually.[36] Clubs could lose upwards of a third of that from 2020 alone. This is by no means good, but things didn't go as bad as people thought. The efforts to resume the sport, albeit for imperialistic and capitalistic reasons, as soon as it did kept it from being a crisis.

There is a report from the European Club Association (ECA) that projects four billion pounds[37] worth of lower revenues, across Europe's top 20 top-flight leagues over two seasons. That's a lot of money but COVID was a strange year, and many people have moaned about the money in the sport. That's from a profit of 41 billion the year before and non-COVID years.

This is all without eyes on stadium sponsorship, merchandise and hospitality, all-important revenue streams for the clubs. With people out of work, those figures drop. Plus, we see television contracts trying to cut their ties because of a lack of money. The lucky thing in all of this was that world sport, and the governing bodies, made sure to

---

36 https://resources.fifa.com/image/upload/fifa-2019-2022-revised-budget.pdf?cloudid=f8brxvwdbs8npinqagg8

37 www.ecaeurope.com/media/4771/eca_covid-19-financial-impact-on-european-clubs.pdf

end the 2019/20 season. That completion worldwide saved money for the clubs as they didn't have to break contracts, and they got the full allotment of money a full season would have got. The 2020/21 season started late, but they could get the sports calendar in for the year.

Thanks from the Author

THERE ARE so many people to thank when writing a book. Fortunately, this is my sophomore effort. Above everything, I want to thank my father, Richard Brandt, who helped nurture my love for the sport, and is always willing to listen to me drone on about some random fact on Flamengo that seems earth-shattering to me at the time. My good friends Mateo and Amanda Escobar, who have always been fans. Duffy Alverson, who has been my co-host on the Subs Bench, releasing all your podcasting applications for almost five years. Also I have to give credit to Marcelo Barreto, for helping me with some of the historical facts behind the book. He was the guy who got me thinking about this, and hopefully this book will be worth the read for him.

I want to thank Jane Camillin at Pitch Publishing for helping me with this project.

Some other people who have helped me on this book need thanks too: Stuart Horsfield of *These Football Times* and author of the book *1982 Brazil: The Glorious Failure*; Gary Thacker, author of many books and also with *These Football Times*; Chris Lee, of *Outside Write* and *Origin Stories*, a book published by Pitch Publishing; Aaron Rozek; Jerry Mancini, a Lazio fan; Dan Williamson, an author and first-team manager; and David Goldblatt, who wrote the bible of soccer history, *The Ball is Round*. I do also want to thank anyone who has written, podcasted or started a Twitter account on Brazilian football; your research and help, unbeknown to you, was a massive help.

Furthermore, I want to thank Flamengo, Zico and the South American football culture for providing me with the information to write the book. Flamengo in the English-speaking world are still vastly underrepresented. In the age of deep-dive blogs, and *These Football Times*, the lack of Flamengo content in English is shocking. Flamengo has a great history, as we have seen.

Appendix

It's one thing to read about the matches and the seasons, but with so much being filmed, we can provide you with the visuals of the time. Most of the videos will be from Brazil and in Portuguese. Here's a list of the videos to supplement the reading.

Flamengo:
Champions of Brazil – Zico, Nunes, Júnior, among others – YouTube
Sixth Goal (Andrade), in the voice of Jorge Curl, Flamengo 6-0 Botafogo – YouTube
Flamengo – 3 Titles in 21 Days – YouTube

The Intercontinental Cup:
1981 – Liverpool versus Flamengo, 0-3 highlights – YouTube

Copa Libertadores:
1981 – 20 November – Cobreloa (Chile) 1-0 Flamengo – YouTube
1981 – Flamengo 1-0 Dep Cali – YouTube
2019 – Flamengo 2-1 River Plate – YouTube

Fla–Flu:
Flamengo 5-2 Fluminense, 1972 – YouTube

Bibliography

Bellos, Alex, *Futebol: Soccer, the Brazilian Way* (New York City: Bloomsbury, 2002).

Brandt, Stephen, *Boca Juniors: A History and Appreciation of Buenos Aires' Most Successful Fútol Team* (Virginia: Mascot Books, 2020).

Campomar, Andreas, *Golazo!* (New York City: Riverhead Books, 2014).

Foer, Franklin, *How Soccer Explains the World* (New York City: HarperCollins, 2006).

Goldblatt, David, *The Ball is Round: A Global History of Soccer* (New York City: Riverhead Books, 2008).

Goldblatt, David, *Futebol Nation: The Story of Brazil through Soccer* (New York City: Bold Type Books, 2014).

Horsfield, Stuart, *1982 Brazil: The Glorious Failure* (Sussex: Pitch Publishing, 2020).

Hughes, Simon, *Red Machine: Liverpool FC in the 1980s* (London: Mainstream Publishing, 2013).

Hughes, Simon, *There She Goes: Liverpool, a City on Its Own: The Long Decade 1979–1993* (London: deCoubertin Books, 2019).

Hylland, Christopher, *Tears at La Bombonera* (Sussex: Pitch Publishing, 2021).

Kelly, Richard, *Keegan and Dalglish* (London: Simon & Schuster, 2017).

Kittleson, Roger, *The Country of Football: Soccer and the Making of Modern Brazil. Volume 2.* (Berkeley: University of California Press, 2014).

Lee, Chris, *Origin Stories* (Sussex: Pitch Publishing, 2021).

Thacker, Gary, *Beautiful Bridesmaids Dressed in Organje: The Unfulfilled Glory Of Dutch Football* (Sussex: Pitch Publishing, 2021).

These Football Times, *Celtic* (London: These Football Times, 2020).

These Football Times, *Liverpool* (London: These Football Times, 2020).

Whiting, Jim, *Flamengo* (Minnesota: The Creative Company, 2018).

Wilson, Jonathan, *Angels with Dirty Faces: How Argentinian Soccer Defined a Nation and Changed the Game Forever* (New York City: Nation Books, 2016).

Wilson, Jonathan, *Inverting the Pyramid: The History of Soccer Tactics.* Fully revised and updated. (New York City: Nation Books, 2018).

Internet Sources

These Football Times Online

Flamengo Alternativo

Soccervoice – Football blogging

World Soccer Talk

Natter Football

Forbes

The Independent

No Win Rio

The Good Schools Guide

LFChistory.net

The Brasilivero
Vavel
World Soccer
The Football Pink
The Versed
Sky Sports
Americas Quarterly
GiveMeSport
Box to Box Football
A Nação
Storie di Calcio
Sports Illustrated